GARIBALDI

THE MAN AND THE MYTH

Donn Byrne

And one man in his time plays many parts.
William Shakespeare

*I have lived a very tempestuous life
which, like most people's, has been a mixture
of good and bad. However, I have always tried
to do good . . . and if I have ever done wrong,
it certainly wasn't intentional.*
Giuseppe Garibaldi *Memoirs* **(1872)**

ISBN 0–906149–99–1

Typesetting and make up: *Katerprint Typesetting Services, Oxford*

Printed in Hong Kong

All photographs reproduced by permission of the BBC Hulton Picture Library. Cover photograph, 'Resa di Palermo', from a private collection, Milan.

Contents

What people said about him . . .

As I have often remarked, Garibaldi is born to command.
Gustav Hoffstetter

You have only to look into his face to feel that here is the one man you would follow blindfold to death. **Harriet Meuricoffre**

You know the face of a lion? Isn't it a foolish face? Well, isn't that the face of Garibaldi? **Giuseppe Mazzini**

There is magic in his look . . . and in his name.
Giuseppe Abba

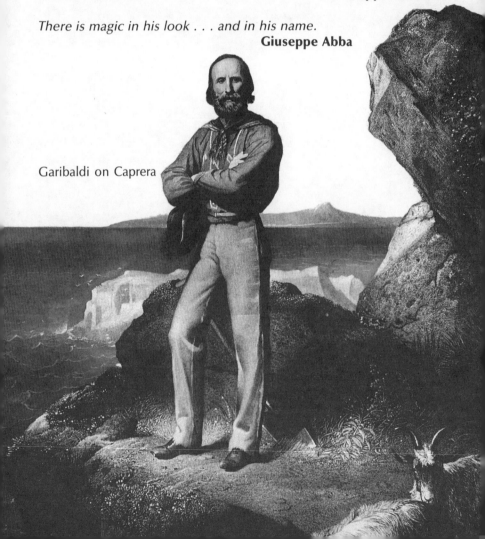

Garibaldi on Caprera

1
The Dying Hero

His time had come, he reckoned, but he felt no regret or resentment. He'd grown tired of the constant struggle against ill health.

First the arthritis that had twisted arms and legs, making a mockery of a man of action. And now this congestion that made every breath an agony. Easier to untie the knot and let the boat drift away.

And besides, seventy-five years was a long voyage for a man.

Of course he'd be sorry to leave them, especially Francesca. A good woman she'd turned out to be. Thank God he'd held out against Teresita's displeasure. She hadn't liked the idea of her father taking up with the children's nurse!

Yes, a good woman, even though she was no beauty. She'd understood him, unlike most of the others. No doubt about it, he'd been a fool over women. Except for Anita.

Anita . . . spied through a telescope and carried off casually, another man's wife, to be his companion in arms. Had he brought her to her death in Magnavacca, or was it her own nagging jealousy, her fear of being abandoned?

It was Rio Grande he thought of so often these days . . . the white stallions and the great black bulls on the pampas; and the antelopes and ostriches. And the dawns and sunsets over the plains and the forests.

Anita had shared the pleasure and pain of the battles that had made him. And he'd taken her to her death . . . a last ride on a bullock cart.

Odd, though, that his first and last love had been a Francesca. But that was another story!

Well, he'd try to hang on for another month for his birthday. (They'd have had a day of celebrations for it in Montevideo!) Yes, he'd hang on if only to please Francesca, who liked to make a fuss of him that day. And, to tell the truth, he didn't mind being made a fuss of either, these days.

This room, where he spent his days, with a view straight onto the sea, had been her idea. Her birthday present a couple of years ago. She'd fixed the whole lot herself, even hiring the masons.

And all the while the work was being done she'd lied to him. Told him she was having a door at the back of the house made bigger, so that they could take his bed outside in the hot weather.

He'd half guessed something else was going on, hearing the noise week in, week out. But all he could think about was the expense. But she'd fixed that side of it too, peasant that she was! The room had to be finished for his birthday or the workmen wouldn't get a penny!

Well, when the day came, she dragged him backwards into the room in his wheelchair. And then he understood what all the noise had been about! There was a high iron bed, too, so that he could see out of the window. And gardenias everywhere – his favourite flower!

And as if that wasn't enough, the band struck up at that moment. Silly old fool that he was, he just burst into tears! Well, at his age you couldn't always control your feelings.

Of course the children were in on it as well, Clelia and Manlio. He'd be sorry to leave them too, though he'd never loved them like the two Rositas. Still, he'd managed to give them his name in the end and to make an honest woman out of Francesca.

Well, the family should be all right here on Caprera. Maybe the government would even give them a pension. After all, he'd refused one often enough for himself.

Clelia, little plainface, would need something. And Manlio, well, perhaps he could go into the navy. And maybe make a better job of his life than his father!

And as for politics, well, he'd finished with that a long time back. He'd done his bit for 'Italy' and more than enough, handing them Sicily and Naples on a plate. Scant gratitude they'd shown him for that! The king had got most of the glory, and the court historians had even tried to write him out of the history books!

Oh, they'd offered him honours and rewards by the yard of course! But who wants a castle and a steamship when you have Caprera! Instead, when he'd asked to be made governor of the south, they'd turned him down.

After all, he was only a self-made pirate with the brains of an ox!

And they'd gone on to make a mess of it themselves. Italy, his dream, had become an illusion, a nightmare. And would remain so until these men from the north could understand the southerners.

And one day, no doubt, people would blame it all on him, Garibaldi!

As for what was left of himself, his twisted body, he'd made all the right provisions. He'd never liked the idea of being buried in the

2

ground, anyway, to provide fodder for worms. There was something unnatural about it.

No, the only decent thing was to be burnt in the open air. Not cremated, mind you, which was like being baked in an oven. Burnt in the open air, with your face turned upwards towards the sun. Like one of the Greek heroes, all dressed in armour.

Except that he'd be wearing his red shirt as usual . . .

Well, he'd chosen the place, that hollow a few hundred yards from the house. And he'd chosen the wood too, from the acacia tree that burnt like oil.

Pity he couldn't choose the exact time too . . . But that would be asking too much!

Giuseppe Garibaldi died at 6.30 pm on June 2 1882, a month before his seventy-fifth birthday.

2
The Student

In the year 1815 a small boy sat on a hillside overlooking Nice, book in hand, gazing dreamily out to sea. Napoleon had just gone into exile on St Helena and the boy and his family had once more become subjects of the King of Sardinia.

But the boy wasn't thinking about the recent events of history, and the book he was holding remained unread. He was absorbed in the sea and his head buzzed with stories which the sailors in the port had told him: about magical distant places . . . Constantinople and Odessa in the east . . . Barcelona and Gibraltar in the west.

His parents wanted him to be a lawyer, a doctor . . . or even a priest! The boy smiled to himself at the idea. Of course it would never happen!

For he had already decided that one day he would be a sailor . . .

Giuseppe Maria Garibaldi was born in the seaport of Nice on July 4 1807. Nice at that time was part of France, as it is today, and the young Garibaldi was in fact christened 'Joseph Marie'. Thus, for the first few years of his life, until Nice was restored to the Kingdom of Sardinia in 1815, this most famous of Italians was a French subject of the Emperor Napoleon and grew up speaking French.

But in other respects Garibaldi was 'Italian'. Both his parents — his father, Domenico Garibaldi, and his mother, Rosa Raimondi — had come to Nice from Liguria, in the north of Italy, and within the family they still spoke the dialect of that area. Many Italians in Nice, Garibaldi complains in his autobiography, forgot that they were Italian. Garibaldi never did.

Domenico Garibaldi — 'a sailor and the son of a sailor' — was a sea captain and owned a small sailing ship of about thirty tons, the *Santa Reparata* (named after the patron saint of Nice), in which he used to carry cargo, mostly oil and wine, along the coast.

It was a hard life and Domenico, it seems, never made a great deal of money. He had inherited the *Santa Reparata* from his father, but he never owned a house of his own. The family lodged first with an uncle of Rosa's, and later, when Garibaldi was seven, moved into rooms in a large tenement house called Maison Aburarum on the quayside.

Besides, Domenico had a large family to support. Apart from Giuseppe — known as 'Peppino' in the family — there were three other sons and a daughter called Teresa, who died in a fire at the age of three. In his autobiography, Garibaldi tells us very little about his childhood. 'Nothing very remarkable happened!' he says. But he writes affectionately of his parents, who were pious conventional people, especially his mother. 'She could be the model of all mothers,' he says of her. She was, it appears, inclined to be a little overprotective towards her second son, who was perhaps already showing signs of a strong will.

Shortage of money at home may also explain why young Garibaldi did not go to a regular school. All the same, his parents had ambitions for their son and engaged a number of teachers for him.

"Perhaps he could be a lawyer . . . or even a priest," Rosa told her husband. "At any rate, he's not going to be a sailor like the rest of the family!"

And so Peppino was taught to read and write; he learnt proper Italian too, some Latin — and even a little English! "I wish I'd paid more attention to it," he remarked later in life, after he had had a good deal to do with English people.

History he enjoyed, too, especially Roman history. But it was mathematics he was really interested in, and geography and astronomy — anything to do with the sea! He was even prepared to study on his own if necessary . . . in order to become a sailor!

Along with his friends of the neighbourhood, Giuseppe spent a good deal of time on the waterfront, close to his home, on and off the ships that filled the harbour; and it was here too that he completed his 'practical education' — something he attached a great deal of importance to in later life. He learnt how to tie knots and fix sails and went on short sailing trips with some of his sailor friends.

"If you want to be a sailor, start young!" he argued, remembering his own early days. "Even at the age of eight! There's no point in studying in Milan or Paris until you're twenty!"

And in the harbour he also listened to sailors' tales, which excited him to travel, and heard for the first time songs which he was later able to sing so well.

Also, early in life, he learnt to swim. In fact he says he could never remember actually *learning* — which perhaps is not surprising for a boy who had grown up on the waterfront. At any rate he must have been a good swimmer by the age of eight when he claims to have rescued a washerwoman from drowning. She had fallen headfirst

5

into a deep ditch of water and, small as he was, Peppino dived in to save her. This was the first of many occasions on which he played the hero by saving someone's life.

Thus, for most of his boyhood, the young Garibaldi led a happy outdoor life, though with a reputation for being a bit of a dreamer, often to be found absorbed in a book. He may not even have been such a bad student after all — perhaps just reluctant to study things that did not interest him — and determined *not* to become a lawyer or a priest.

He showed this determination when he and some boys stole a boat and began to sail towards Genoa, without any clear idea of where they would go after that. Luckily they were caught and brought home — informed on by a young priest. 'For once a priest did me a good turn!' Garibaldi comments, because he probably saved the boys' lives.

Perhaps this escapade was the turning-point that made his parents realise that it was no use trying to keep their son from going to sea. In any case, on November 12 1821, when he was just fourteen, Giuseppe finally got his wish and was enrolled as a sailor — as a cabin boy.

But it was not until two years later that he was finally allowed to go on his first long sea voyage to one of the distant ports he had heard so many stories about — Odessa!

3
The Seaman

At last his dream was coming true!

His mother handed him his bundle of clothes and kissed him goodbye. His father clapped him gruffly on the back, gave him a few last words of advice (not that he had ever got as far as Odessa!) and led his wife, still weeping, back to the quay.

The boy waved as the ship began to move, impatient to be off. Then Nice faded into the early morning mist and they were on their way to the east.

"Oh how beautiful this ship is!" he murmured to himself as he gazed about him.

A voice broke in upon his daydreams. It was the ship's mate. "Come along, then, young Garibaldi! Look sharp! There's work to be done on this ship. You'll never get to be a sailor this way!"

Garibaldi finally went to sea in January 1824, when he travelled on the brigantine *Costanza* to the Russian port of Odessa. It must have seemed like one long exciting adventure for him, sailing down the coast of Italy, across the Aegean and finally into the Black Sea.

Not surprisingly, he loved his first ship and in his sketchy account of his early voyages he described it in some detail, with its broad sides, its wide decks and a prow 'shaped like a woman'. He had great praise for the captain too, Angelo Pesante. 'The best sea captain I have ever known!' he wrote of him in his autobiography.

Garibaldi was away from home for just over six months. He never sailed on the *Costanza* again but he managed to keep in touch with Angelo Pesante throughout much of his life.

The *Costanza*, like other ships in the Mediterranean at that time, was a sailing ship of about two hundred tons, with a crew of around a dozen sailors. From the ports of Nice, Marseilles and Genoa these ships usually carried a cargo of wine, oil or sugar to the Levant and brought back grain or flour from South Russia.

It was on ships like these that Garibaldi learnt to be tough and practical over the next nine years — and this gave him a great advantage over many of his fellow-revolutionaries in later years. He rose quite rapidly from cabin boy to first mate and finally got his master's certificate — second class — in 1831.

Physically, at the time, it would seem that he was not especially striking. He was rather short — about five foot six inches tall — and broad shouldered. His hair and his beard (which perhaps he grew later) were a chestnut colour, and his eyes were dark-brown (not blue, as was sometimes said later on). He had a fresh, healthy complexion and was also reputed to be fussy about his personal cleanliness. Otherwise he had no special features.

He did, however, have a good tenor voice and he enjoyed singing. Later he used his voice to good effect as a speaker, especially to put courage into his troops. But he had not yet developed the magnetic personality and charismatic appearance (reminding many of Christ) which attracted those who came in contact with him later in life — even those ready to dislike him.

On his return from Odessa, Garibaldi worked for a time on his father's ship. In the same year they went on a short voyage along the French coast and in March of the following year as far as Rome: 1825 was a Holy Year, though Domenico Garibaldi also had other business in Rome.

They stayed there for over a month, so the young Garibaldi had plenty of time to explore the city which until then he had only read about in history books. It made a great impression on him, this city of priests and ruins. Writing about the visit twenty-five years later, he claimed that he had seen not only Rome of the past, in all its former glory, but also Rome of the future — the symbol of a united Italy.

It is perhaps unlikely that he had such a clear-cut vision at the time, but this dream of a united Italy, with Rome as the capital, later became an obsession with him.

Over the next few years Garibaldi continued to travel regularly both to Mediterranean ports and into the Black Sea. Only once, it seems, did he go past Gibraltar into the Atlantic. This was in 1827, when he sailed as far as the Canary Islands. About this time, too, he had his first taste of fighting, when his ship was attacked three times by pirates.

These 'pirates' were mostly Greek revolutionaries who, after Greece rebelled against Turkey in 1821, used to attack Turkish shipping in the Aegean. But they sometimes attacked neutral ships too and, although he later became a kind of pirate himself in South America, Garibaldi had little sympathy for them at the time. If his account of what happened to his ship is true, he was lucky to have escaped with his life!

On one of these trips to the Levant, Garibaldi fell ill and had to be left behind in Constantinople. When he recovered, war had broken out between Turkey and Russia and there was no way he could return home. Stranded without money in Constantinople for at least a year, he had to find some way of supporting himself. Rather surprisingly, perhaps, since he had been only too glad to turn his back on lessons, he took up teaching and worked as a tutor to the three young children of an Italian widow.

He also began to learn Greek on his own account — which, he says, he soon forgot, like the little Latin he had learnt as a child. Perhaps with his growing interest in political events, this study of Greek was not just a way of passing the time but also reflected his admiration for the Greek struggle for independence, especially the guerrilla leaders.

One interesting consequence of Garibaldi's prolonged stay in Constantinople was that he failed to get married at this point of his life. For, before he had left for the Black Sea, he had fallen in love with a girl called Francesca Roux. The two had become engaged, no doubt intending to marry on Garibaldi's return home. So when he finally returned to Nice, he rushed round to Francesca's house, even jumping over the wall into the garden in his eagerness to see her. He found Francesca there — but she was not alone: she was nursing a baby. Also, he noticed, she was wearing a wedding-ring! Francesca started to explain.

"I'm sorry, Peppino . . . "

"It's all right!" Garibaldi told her. "I understand! Be happy!" Then he turned and left without another word.

So perhaps in her own small way Francesca Roux changed the course of Garibaldi's life — and history! For he was now on the point of making a voyage of great importance — one that would bring him into contact with ideas that would change his whole outlook and determine the course of his life from now on. If Garibaldi had married at this point and settled down, he might never have become a rebel and a revolutionary.

4
The Conspirator

He wasn't on duty that night but he waited up on deck with the rest of the crew to see their passengers come aboard. It wasn't just out of curiosity. He had hardly glanced at the reports of their trial which had filled all the papers. And he certainly wasn't amused by the jokes which the crew had been making about them for days past.

The captain, no fool, noticed his interest and began to tease him, slyly.

"I'd keep clear of that lot, Peppino, if I were you! You've got enough soft ideas in your head as it is! They'll land you in trouble one of these days."

He nodded and smiled, not wishing to get into an argument with the captain at that time of night. Besides, they were coming on board now, heads held high, still singing.

It was then that he knew he must speak to them. There was, he felt sure now, something he had to learn from them . . .

In 1833 Garibaldi signed on as mate for his third voyage on the *Clorinda* and shortly before the ship sailed from Marseilles on March 22, a band of strangely dressed people came on board. They had sung as they passed through the streets, which even at three in the morning were crowded with curious spectators. These new passengers were the Saint-Simonians, who had recently been on trial in Paris and were now going into exile.

The Saint-Simonians were the followers of the French socialist aristocrat, Count de Saint-Simon, who had preached a doctrine of universal love mixed with social equality; of equal distribution of wealth under a government run by businessmen and scientists. After his death in 1825, the movement continued under his successor, Enfantin, and it was then it began to achieve some notoriety.

The Saint-Simonians wore colourful clothes, preached and practised free love and lived in a kind of commune. But their ideas soon began to offend the morality of the age and in 1832 they were arrested and put on trial. Enfantin was sent to prison; thirteen of his followers were sentenced to be banished. It was these who now joined the *Clorinda* under the leadership of Emile Barrault.

Barrault, famous as a writer and a teacher, was as good a talker as Garibaldi was a ready listener, and throughout the long voyage to the Levant there were plenty of opportunities, especially on deck at the end of a long day, 'beneath a sky full of stars', for Barrault to expound the beliefs of this strange sect to an attentive Garibaldi.

Unfortunately — afraid perhaps of boring his readers, who were more likely to be interested in accounts of his battles than in philosophical ideas — Garibaldi tells us next to nothing in his autobiography about what he learnt from the Saint-Simonians. But their ideas clearly made a deep impression on him and appealed to his romantic imagination — especially the importance of fighting for freedom: for another's country, not just one's own. And throughout his life he somehow managed to keep a signed copy of a book which Barrault had given him.

Up to this time, perhaps because he had spent so much of his adult life at sea, Garibaldi had escaped any direct involvement in politics, although, like any other young man of the time, he must have been concerned about the condition of his country.

After the defeat of Napoleon in 1815, Italy — which the Austrian Chancellor Metternich had called a 'mere geographical expression' — had once more been divided into a number of states, all more or less directly or indirectly under the influence of Austria. Their governments, too, were to varying degrees repressive, not least in the states governed by the Pope, who was determined, by putting a stop to political and social progress, that nothing like the French Revolution should ever happen again.

However, the struggle for liberty, and for the broader goal of Italian unity, went on. Secret societies were formed. In 1821, and again in 1831, revolutions broke out — and were brutally suppressed. At some point Garibaldi must have decided that he could no longer stay detached from politics. And so, he says, he began to read all he could find about the Italian struggle for liberty.

Thus, when the *Clorinda* docked in Taganrog in April 1833 (having left the Saint-Simonians in Constantinople, where they hoped to find a new home), Garibaldi was ready for his second encounter, which would lead him to play a more active part in politics.

The encounter took place in a seaman's club in Taganrog, where Garibaldi heard a young man — he calls him a 'young Ligurian', without ever mentioning his name — making a passionate speech about the liberation of Italy and about a movement called 'Young Italy', which the revolutionary leader Mazzini had recently founded.

Mazzini, only two years older than Garibaldi, had become a revolutionary early in life. As a student in Genoa he had joined the secret society of the Carbonari, which preached revolution without, however, ever achieving much. Betrayed to the secret police, Mazzini went into exile and founded his own secret society, which he called 'Young Italy'.

Although an intellectual and an idealist, Mazzini wanted to do something more than just *talk* about revolution. The aim of the new movement was both *national* — to establish a free and independent Italy — and *international* — to win freedom for their fellow-men. These were ideals that coincided very nicely with what Garibaldi had just heard from the Saint-Simonians.

For Garibaldi, this meeting with the 'young Ligurian' was as momentous as 'Columbus discovering America' and, although he was now well on the way to becoming a successful sea captain, he decided that he must risk his career to help his country.

Later, therefore, when he left Taganrog, he took with him the names and addresses of revolutionary contacts in Marseilles.

Back in Marseilles, Garibaldi lost no time in following up the contacts which he had been given. He joined 'Young Italy', almost certainly using a pseudonym, and took the oath of allegiance. Later on, when both he and Mazzini became famous, the two men were often depicted as meeting on that occasion; but in the summer of 1833 it is almost certain that Mazzini was elsewhere.

As so often in his life, Garibaldi was in the right place at the right time. There was work for someone like him, with experience of handling men. A revolution was being planned for the following year. A small army of about eight hundred revolutionaries, entering from Switzerland, was to invade Savoy, which was part of the Kingdom of Sardinia. The invasion was to be accompanied by a revolution in Genoa, supported in turn by a mutiny in the navy.

This was where Garibaldi came in. He was to join the Genovese navy — he was due to do his national service about this time — and, when he was posted to a ship, prepare the way for a mutiny by finding sympathisers among the crew. It seemed a task for which he was ideally suited, since he had lived and worked with sailors.

So, late in December, Garibaldi joined the navy (as a sailor, third class), and was posted to the warship *Eurydice*. The revolution had been planned for the beginning of February and Garibaldi at once set about the task of finding sympathisers for the mutiny. In his enthusiasm, he even carried on the work ashore.

Unfortunately, there were spies everywhere and Garibaldi talked about his work to one of them. From then on, he was a marked man and on February 3 he suddenly found himself transferred to the admiral's flagship. Separated from his friends and under the watchful eye of the authorities, Garibaldi was no longer in a position to start a mutiny.

By then the projected invasion of Savoy had failed—even before it had got properly underway. Only about two hundred of the mercenaries turned up. Mazzini and the military commander of the operation, General Ramorino, began to quarrel. Mazzini, in any case, was no soldier and, on a bitterly cold night in the middle of winter, had come without an overcoat. Ramorino called the invasion off and Mazzini was forced to return to Geneva. It was the first of his many failed revolutions.

News of the fiasco soon reached Genoa, causing confusion among the plotters. Garibaldi, isolated on his new ship, concluded that the game was up, and decided to desert. He found shelter with a friendly fruitseller named Teresina, who also gave him a suit of her husband's clothes. He wasted no time in getting away and, as he was leaving the city, he heard that the police were looking for a sailor called Garibaldi.

Ten days later, having followed an indirect route across the mountains, he reached his parents' home in Nice. His mother especially was shocked at what had happened and blamed everything on the Saint-Simonians. "They have ruined my son!" she was heard to exclaim. When he left home a few days later, Garibaldi was not to see his mother again for another twelve years. His father Domenico, who died in 1842, he never saw again.

Garibaldi knew that he might be arrested at any moment in Nice, so he decided to cross the frontier and go to Marseilles, where other revolutionaries lived without too much interference from the police. He took the identity (as well as the papers) of an English sailor called Joseph Pane and not long afterwards he read in the papers about a trial in Genoa, in which he and two other sailors had been sentenced to death for treason. 'It was the first time I saw my name in the papers,' he wrote with innocent vanity.

After a while he went to sea again, signing on under the name of Joseph Pane, and was away for the whole winter in the Black Sea. On his return, he helped deliver a ship to the Bey of Tunis and then, in the summer of 1835, he worked for a while as an ambulanceman during a cholera epidemic in Marseilles.

It was a dangerous job to take on. Perhaps he needed the money, though more likely this was one of his heroic gestures, like saving someone from drowning. Of this there is yet another example recorded about this time, when he rescued a young boy — diving into the harbour in his best clothes!

But Garibaldi had now decided to leave Europe for South America. His name had been struck off the seaman's register, so he could no longer hope to get work as a captain or as a mate, even in France. Nor, unless there was a change of regime, would he ever be able to return to Nice.

In any case it was quite common at this time to emigrate to the United States or to South America. Garibaldi chose Brazil, perhaps because he thought he would be more at home with the Italian community of Rio, many of whose members were exiles like himself. It is likely that, once again, he had been given the names of contacts there.

Early in September Garibaldi joined a French ship called the *Nautonnier*, still under the assumed name of Joseph Pane. It would seem that he did the work of a mate, without, however, being fully paid for it.

It was 5000 miles to Rio and Garibaldi probably arrived there late in November. Summer was just beginning and his first sight of the city must have filled him with delight.

5
The Pirate

*So where had it all gone wrong, this revolution that was to herald in
a free and united Italy?*

*Not in Genoa, at any rate, and least of all on the Eurydice, where
he'd done his work so well that there was hardly a sailor who hadn't
been willing to join the cause.*

*And yet, in the end, it had come to nothing — and he'd had to run
for it like a common criminal, dressed in another man's clothes. It
was that old drunkard Ramorino who'd let them down, he and that
highbrow Mazzini.*

*Mazzini of course was comfortable enough in Geneva, while he,
Joseph Pane alias Giuseppe Garibaldi, was having to work as a mate
for less than a mate's pay. No chance now of becoming a ship's
captain, with his name struck off the register.*

*Well, he'd made his choice. It was Rio. Better to try his luck in
South America than live from hand to mouth as an exile in Marseilles
for the rest of his life. At least there was hope in Brazil. He might
make some money, or find a cause to fight for.*

*And, who knows, one day he might even be pardoned and
allowed to go back home . . .*

It did not take Garibaldi long to find a cause to fight for. The
province of Rio Grande in the south of Brazil had recently broken
away and declared itself a republic under the leadership of Bento
Gonçalves. Gonçalves himself was soon defeated and imprisoned in
Rio, together with his Italian secretary, Count Tito Zambeccari, but
the struggle for independence went on. It was exactly the kind of
cause to capture the romantic imagination of Garibaldi!

He had lost no time in making contact with other Italian exiles,
who in any case had heard of his part in the abortive revolution of
Genoa. He joined the local branch of 'Young Italy' and wrote some
articles attacking the King of Sardinia in the local newspaper — all of
which was duly reported back by the king's minister in Rio.

Not content with this, he also wrote to Mazzini, asking for authority to attack Piedmontese shipping as a 'pirate'. It was not a request

that Mazzini was in a position to grant, and Garibaldi got no reply to his letter.

For the best part of a year, together with Luigi Rossetti, an Italian journalist he had met when he first arrived in Rio, he tried his hand at commerce. But their efforts at coastal trading met with no great success. People cheated them and, in any case, Garibaldi could never give himself wholeheartedly to anything intended solely to make money.

Besides, he wanted to do something for 'the cause', as he told a fellow-member of 'Young Italy' in Montevideo, Giambattista Cuneo (whom many believe to be the 'young Ligurian' he met in Taganrog).

'Write to Pippo' (this was Mazzini's pet name), 'tell him to give us a prescription and we will get it made up. I am tired of dragging on this life of a trading sailor, so useless to our country.'

Garibaldi longed to be a conspirator again!

It was at this point, early in 1837, that Garibaldi became involved in Rio Grande's struggle for independence — perhaps through Zambeccari, who was also a member of 'Young Italy'. Once again he proposed to become an authorised 'pirate', with the object this time of attacking Brazilian shipping on behalf of the Rio Grande government. The rebels, who had no navy of their own, were intrigued by his proposal, and his request was granted. After all, they had nothing to lose from Garibaldi's enterprise.

Almost as soon as he left Rio, in a 20-tonner called the *Mazzini* in honour of the master, Garibaldi captured a Brazilian ship, the *Luisa*, carrying a cargo of coffee. The *Luisa* was larger than his own vessel, so he took it over, having set the crew free in one of the boats.

He had started well, but he had one pressing problem: he urgently needed provisions. Since the Brazilian navy was successfully blockading the ports of Rio Grande, Garibaldi decided to sail south, as far as Uruguay, where he put in at Maldonado.

It took time to dispose of their captured cargo. Rossetti, who had joined him in this venture, went to Montevideo to try to arrange for the coffee to be sold there, and in the meantime Garibaldi himself was pleasantly entertained ashore. Then, out of the blue, came the news that the Uruguayans (who, it had been assumed, were friendly towards Rio Grande) had given the Brazilians permission to retake the ship.

Garibaldi had to leave Maldonado in a hurry, though not before he had claimed at pistol point some money owed to him by a local merchant. His only sure way of escape from the Brazilians was to sail up the River Plate. But, as he was passing Montevideo, two Uruguayan gunboats opened fire on the ship.

In the battle that followed, Garibaldi, in his own words, was 'mortally wounded' by a bullet in the neck. Even so he managed to instruct his inexperienced crew to sail up the River Paraná, where in ten days they reached the small Argentine port of Gualaguay.

The Argentine authorities impounded both the ship and the cargo, later handing them back to their Brazilian owners. The crew, however, were allowed to leave, with the exception of Garibaldi. As the person responsible for organising this act of piracy, the government in Buenos Aires needed time to decide what to do with him.

In the meantime he was well looked after. Once he had recovered from his wound, for which he was treated by the governor's personal surgeon, he was allowed to live in a private house and was even given a daily allowance. But he had to give his word that he would not try to escape.

Thus Garibaldi spent the next few months pleasantly enough, learning Spanish and, crucial for his future career, learning how to ride. But he resented his confinement. 'I wanted to be free!' he protested in his memoirs, and when he heard he was going to be transferred to the capital of the province, he decided to break his word and try to escape.

He was recaptured the following day — afterwards he wondered if he was really *meant* to escape — and was brutally tortured to try to make him confess who had helped him. It was an experience he could not talk about for the rest of his life without a shudder. Then, two months later, he was suddenly set free and allowed to make his own way back to Montevideo.

When Garibaldi finally got back to Rio Grande in the middle of 1838, he spent some time with General Bento Gonçalves, who in the meantime had managed to escape from prison in Rio. Gonçalves was a colourful personality, a simple but heroic man fighting for ideals, though he was rarely very lucky in war. Garibaldi developed a great admiration for him and Gonçalves almost certainly served as a model for him in later years.

The Rio Grandenses had work for Garibaldi to do. He was put in charge of the 'navy', which at the time consisted of a mere two ships and about seventy men. With this small force he and his companion in arms, the American John Griggs, managed to inflict a good deal of damage on Brazilian shipping, even though he was confined in a lagoon, the Lagoa dos Patos, by their blockade.

Garibaldi was beginning to make his name, not just as a 'pirate' —

17

he had already earned the nickname of the 'The Devil' — but also as a skilful commander and fighter.

About this time he had his first taste of fighting on land, in a skirmish with a particularly cunning Brazilian commander, and had good reason to be proud of his success, which he describes in great detail in his memoirs. For, with just a handful of men, he succeeded in beating off a raiding party of over one hundred and fifty attackers.

The following year, in 1839, the Rio Grandenses decided to attack Santa Catarina, the province to the north, where a republican revolt against Rio was also planned. The main target of rebel operations was the city of Laguna, and Garibaldi's role was to provide naval support.

But to do this, he first had to get his two ships out of the Lagoa dos Patos, where they were still confined. Since it was impossible to break through the Brazilian blockade, he had his ships dragged fifty miles across land on huge carts, which were specially built for this purpose and had to be pulled by over two hundred oxen.

This ingenious feat, however, was followed by disaster. His ship got caught in a hurricane and sank, with the loss of most of the crew. But the attack on Laguna went ahead and it was in that city, successfully taken by the Rio Grandense rebels shortly afterwards, that Garibaldi met Anita, the woman who was to be his wife and companion for the next ten years.

By now Brazil was becoming increasingly disturbed at the spread of the revolt in the south and a strong force was sent to win back Santa Catarina, where things were already beginning to go wrong for the new regime. There were revolts by Brazilian supporters, reluctant to be 'liberated' by the Rio Grande forces, who had begun to behave like an occupying army.

Garibaldi himself was sent to suppress one of these revolts, which he did efficiently and thoroughly. But he was disgusted by the way his soldiers behaved, and began to realise for the first time how even a war fought in the name of liberty can be a very unpleasant and brutal affair.

The Brazilian army and navy were now advancing in strength upon Laguna and the Rio Grandenses were forced to withdraw from Santa Catarina. Garibaldi's navy was destroyed and he was obliged to join in the retreat as a soldier, together with Anita. Over the next few months he had his first experience of guerrilla warfare and perhaps began to work out his own basic principles for waging it.

But, although the Rio Grandenses won some victories as they retreated to their own province, their situation was becoming increasingly precarious. Here too they were losing support. Many people had grown tired of the war and wanted to negotiate with the Brazilians, who were now prepared to offer them some measure of self-government.

Gonçalves, however, refused to negotiate and when Brazil sent another force against them, both the army and the government began a long retreat into the interior. During the retreat, across high mountains and in bitterly cold weather, the Rio Grandenses suffered terrible hardships. For Garibaldi and Anita, taking with them their new-born son, it was an exceptionally distressing experience.

Shortly after they reached their permanent camp, Garibaldi asked Gonçalves to release him from the service of Rio Grande (whose struggle was to go on for another five years). He had decided to go to Montevideo, at least for a while, where he hoped to get news of his family, with whom he had been out of touch since he left Rio. No doubt too he was concerned for Anita and his son.

It is possible also that Garibaldi was beginning to grow disillusioned with the so-called struggle for liberty — which seemed to involve killing those who did not support the same cause. Gonçalves gave him permission to leave and also to take a herd of 1000 cattle, which would give him some sort of start for his new life in Montevideo.

And so Garibaldi set off on the 400-mile journey to Montevideo, a very different person from the young exile who had arrived in Rio some six years earlier. He was now an experienced naval commander, with several small victories to his credit, and with some experience of fighting on land too. He had also won a reputation for being a very brave man.

Perhaps most surprising of all, however, for someone who had led an unsettled existence, he also had a family to support.

6
The Lover

He had waited so long — and yet in the end it had been so easy, this business of finding a wife!

One day he had been alone on his ship . . . commander-in-chief of the Rio Grande navy, yes, but all alone and feeling very low with all his mates lost in that storm, and the very next day he had acquired this treasure . . . this pearl beyond price!

And what a treasure! A companion in arms, too, in more than one sense of the word! And to think that she had been rotting away in Laguna, passing her days in gossip and trivial tasks about the house, when all the time she was cut out to be a fighter.

Of course there was talk — there always is — by small-minded people afraid to dare as they had dared. And envious too because a love like theirs offends them. "Another man's wife!" they whisper. "And him away at the front."

Well, let them gossip . . . they'd show them! She might be the target of all the spiteful tongues of Laguna at the moment, but one day, riding at his side, she'd be the toast of all Italy . . . would his Anita!

In his autobiography Garibaldi says he first caught sight of Anita from the deck of the *Itaparica*, a Brazilian ship he had been given after the capture of Laguna to replace the one lost in the hurricane. He was still suffering from a deep depression, brought on by the loss of his Italian friends in the shipwreck, and felt quite alone in the world.

So for the first time in his life he decided to look for a wife — an idea which he says had never occurred to him before because of his temperament and his wandering way of life. He needed an exceptional woman — and quite by chance he found one.

As he gazed at the shore through his telescope, he tells us, he saw a girl working in front of a house. He liked the look of her and decided to go ashore to try to meet her. At first he had no luck as he combed the area and he had almost given up hope of finding the girl when a man he knew invited him into his house for a cup of coffee.

20

And there, inside the house, he saw the girl he had been looking for!

The two stared at each other in a state of ecstasy, unable to say a word, Garibaldi records. It was love at first sight! 'I spoke little Portuguese at the time,' he says (which is perhaps not completely accurate), 'so I addressed her in Italian.'

"*Tu devi esser mia!*" You must be mine!

It was more than enough: the girl understood and agreed. Almost by magic Garibaldi had found the woman of his dreams — the woman who was to be 'the mother of my children . . . the companion of my life in all its ups and downs!'

Garibaldi's account of his meeting with Anita may sound as fantastic as a fairy tale, but there is no reason to disbelieve that this is essentially what happened. Everything is quite in keeping with the impetuous and romantic way Garibaldi behaved then and later in his life in matters of the heart.

Anita Garibaldi, as she eventually became, was born Ana Maria de Jesus. Her father was a poor Brazilian peasant, originally from the province of San Paolo, who had moved further south in search of work, and Anita may well have been of mixed Portuguese and Indian descent. She was probably born in 1821 and was therefore eighteen or nineteen when she met Garibaldi.

After her father's death, her mother had come to live in Laguna. Here, when she was little more than fourteen, Ana Maria was married to a shoemaker called Manoel Duarte (who was perhaps also a fisherman in his spare time).

Manoel was several years older than his bride and seems to have been a dour and very conventional man. Anita had only married him in the first place under pressure from her mother and the couple may not have got on well. She had been married for about four years when Garibaldi appeared on the scene.

It is not clear where Manoel Duarte was at the time. Perhaps Anita simply decided to elope; there were apparently no children from the marriage. The couple may have separated, or else, as is likely, Manoel may have been away doing his military service with the Brazilian army (and perhaps died later, thus making it possible for Garibaldi and Anita to get married in Montevideo).

At all events, Anita showed no hesitation in joining the dashing, handsome foreigner, who as the commander of the Rio Grande navy was already a well-known figure in Laguna. Equally, Garibaldi had no compunction about carrying off another man's wife.

For this action, whatever the precise circumstances, he seems to have felt some remorse when he came to write his memoirs shortly after Anita's death. 'She is dead — and he is avenged!' he wrote. But Garibaldi did not say who 'he' was — and the mystery surrounding Anita's first husband remains.

It is unlikely that Anita was as beautiful as she is often shown in her portraits and described in stories. In any case, Garibaldi seems rarely to have been attracted to beautiful women! She was probably tall and well built, with large dark eyes and long black hair. Her features, however, may well have been coarse and she was also perhaps a little stout.

Garibaldi describes her as vivacious and brave, and she showed her courage by fighting at her husband's side. She also had a strong personality and was inclined to be very jealous of her 'José' — perhaps not without reason. On one occasion, some years later in Montevideo, Garibaldi appeared with his hair cut very short.

"What happened?" his friends all asked him. Garibaldi was by then famous for his long flowing hair.

"Anita thinks I wore it that way to attract all the women, so I cut it off to keep the peace!"

Soon after they met, the Brazilians began their big push to retake Santa Catarina and, in their advance on Laguna, their navy caught Garibaldi's own small fleet by surprise. Garibaldi, together with most of his sailors, was on shore when the Brazilian navy sailed into the harbour. But Anita had remained on board Garibaldi's ship, the *Rio Pardo*. She immediately opened fire on the Brazilian ships with the cannons and in this way encouraged the sailors on board to resist.

Later, when the situation became desperate and it was decided to evacuate Laguna, Anita supervised the landing of supplies — including munitions — from the ships, while Garibaldi provided covering fire. Thus Anita soon demonstrated to Garibaldi that he had found not just a wife but a real companion in arms.

During the retreat from Laguna over the next three months, Anita took part in numerous battles and skirmishes at Garibaldi's side, sometimes also giving first aid on the battlefield. She proved to be an excellent horsewoman. 'She was my treasure!' Garibaldi observed. 'Battles were like a game for her and the hardships of life in the field a mere pastime.'

On one occasion, according to one of the stories he liked to tell about Anita, her horse was killed under her and she was taken prisoner. Yet she somehow managed to escape and travelled over seventy miles on horseback to rejoin her husband, who had already crossed the border into Rio Grande, convinced that she was dead.

In September 1840 their first child was born. He was called Menotti — after Ciro Menotti, the revolutionary from Modena whose execution in 1831 had moved Garibaldi when he was still an ordinary sailor. Menotti had an adventurous life from his very first days: soon after his birth, while Garibaldi was away, Anita had been forced to take refuge from a Brazilian raiding party and to lie hidden for several days in the woods until the Brazilians left.

Numerous women and children took part in the second retreat across the highlands in Rio Grande as the Brazilians made even more determined efforts to reassert their authority over the province. Many died on the way; some were even killed to prevent them from falling into the hands of the enemy.

Menotti was only a month old when the retreat began. Anita and Garibaldi usually carried him in a large handkerchief tied around the neck to form a cradle. Because of the extreme cold, Menotti very nearly died and Garibaldi used to try to keep him warm by breathing on him.

The retreat was a great ordeal for Anita, who, because of her anxiety over Menotti, could no longer fight at her husband's side. But there was still no prospect of peace and, having seen so many families lost in the previous months, she must have been relieved when her husband decided or perhaps agreed to leave Rio Grande in search of a more settled way of life in Montevideo.

She was not to know that there would be a similar but final journey through Italy at her husband's side.

7
The Admiral

Well, the quiet life in Montevideo hadn't lasted for long!

There was work to be done, since these poor fools had got themselves into a fight with a neighbour ten times their size and needed a navy. And who better to put one together than the ex-commander of the Rio Grande fleet, José Garibaldi!

But first he'd been sent on that crazy expedition up the Paraná, which had nearly proved the end of him (and perhaps that was what it was all about! You never knew with some of these politicians!).

But if they thought they'd seen the last of him, someone had got it wrong. He'd held his own against that old Irishman Brown and had more than once got close to blowing up his ships during the night. But in the end it had been his own ships that had been sent sky-high, by his own hand, and perhaps a few drunken sailors with them.

So here he was, once more on his way to Montevideo, where the fat merchants hardly wanted to lift a finger to defend their own city, happy to leave it to others.

But did it matter in the end? Put it all down to experience . . . It would come in handy one day when he finally got back to Italy.

Garibaldi lost most of the cattle he took with him from Rio Grande: many died on the way; the rest he had to kill off. He arrived in Montevideo with 300 hides — the proceeds from which were barely sufficient to set up home for his family — a room and a shared kitchen in a house not far from the port. There he continued to live in near-poverty even after he became commander of the Uruguayan navy.

For some months he earned his living first as a commercial traveller and then for a time as a teacher of mathematics and history in a private school. Early in 1842 he and Anita got married. The reason for their marrying at this stage is not clear: possibly they had got news from Rio Grande that Anita's husband was now dead.

Whatever the reason, Garibaldi was now being dragged back into the arena of war, perhaps not entirely against his will. Another noble 'cause' had presented itself and Garibaldi was too experienced a fighter to be left on one side. Perhaps, too, some of his Italian friends were putting pressure on him to take part.

The new 'cause' was a war between Uruguay and Argentina. This, in part at least, was a civil war between rival political parties within Uruguay itself, where the president of the country, General Rivera, leader of the liberal party, the *colorados*, had not long before driven out his rival and predecessor, General Oribe, who led the conservatives, the *blancos*.

Oribe had taken refuge in neighbouring Argentina and was now trying to regain power with the help of the Argentine dictator, General Manuel Rosas. The conflict was further encouraged by Argentine refugees in Montevideo, who had fled from Rosas' oppressive and often brutal regime and were also opposed to his policy of federal government.

It was a complicated affair but, as so often in his life, Garibaldi saw the issues in simple clear-cut terms: like Rio Grande, Uruguay was a small infant republic struggling for liberty and survival against a tyrant. He was always ready to join in a struggle of that kind.

Early in 1842 Garibaldi was given an appointment in the Uruguayan navy and almost immediately was sent on a mission which only he would have been brave — or perhaps rash — enough to take on.

With a small fleet of three ships and about five hundred men, his task was to slip past the Argentine navy that patrolled the River Plate and then sail 500 miles up the River Paraná, through enemy country, harassing Argentine shipping on the way, until he made contact with Uruguayan supporters in Corrientes in the north.

Luck was on his side when he set off. He managed to get past the Argentine fortress on the island of Martín García and to evade their fleet commanded by the Irishman, Admiral Brown. Then he made his way up the River Paraná, seizing and destroying Argentine shipping *en route* and attacking Argentine towns. It earned him the reputation of being a ruthless pirate.

Brown, meanwhile, had sailed up the River Uruguay in hot pursuit of Garibaldi. It did not cross his mind that his opponent would go up the Paraná, where he could be easily trapped.

Besides, Brown knew something that Garibaldi was not yet aware of: the water-level of the Paraná, never a deep river, was exceptionally low that year. Garibaldi did not appreciate the problem he faced until he reached the town of Costa Brava, some two hundred and fifty miles short of Corrientes, where he was met by some Uruguayan vessels that had come downstream to help him.

There he discovered that he could go no further with his own ships, which were not built for shallow waters. He decided, therefore, to stay and fight, assuming — correctly as it turned out — that Admiral Brown was not far behind.

The battle at Costa Brava lasted for two whole days. Brown soon discovered that he had one great advantage over his opponent: his cannons had a much longer range. All he had to do, therefore, was to keep out of range of Garibaldi's guns while he battered him into submission.

At the end of the first day, August 15, Garibaldi's own ship was so badly damaged that the officer in charge of the Corrientes detachment tried to persuade him to make his escape in their vessels. Garibaldi refused, even though he was already running short of ammunition. He still hoped to destroy the Argentine fleet by surprise attacks under cover of darkness. By the time these attacks had failed, the ships from Corrientes had sailed away and Garibaldi was on his own.

He now had no alternative but to fight on and the battle continued until late afternoon on the following day. When he ran out of ammunition, he loaded his cannons with pieces of chain and lumps of metal.

But by now his ships were almost totally destroyed and over three hundred of his men were dead or dying. He took the only step left to him: he evacuated his ships and blew them up. Then, with his remaining forces, he retreated northwards in the direction of Corrientes and Brown, perhaps because he respected Garibaldi as a fighting man, let him go.

Thus Garibaldi's first big naval engagement ended in defeat, although he had distinguished himself as a fighter. 'We fought only for honour,' he wrote in his autobiography. While the press in Buenos Aires raged against the 'pirate Garibaldi', even accusing him of blowing up his own wounded men, the reports from Montevideo were full of praise for the brave way he had fought against overwhelming odds.

It was without doubt a glorious fight — but it cannot be overlooked that Garibaldi lost most of his men, and little was gained from it except that it raised the morale of the Uruguayans.

After he had got safely away from Costa Brava, Garibaldi spent several months in the north, waiting for instructions from Montevideo. He regarded this period as a waste of time, just as, in retrospect, he regarded the expedition up the Paraná as futile, even

26

half-suspecting that certain people in Montevideo might have sent him on it in order to get rid of him.

Eventually he was given orders to move south to join General Rivera, who was with the Uruguayan army near Paysandu, poised against his opponent Oribe. But Garibaldi arrived too late to take part in the battle of Arroyo Grande, which was fought just across the river from Paysandu. Rivera was heavily defeated, losing most of his army, and the way was now open for Oribe to march on Montevideo.

8
The Leader

More than once — he hadn't dared admit it before — he'd had his doubts, for how can you ever hope to make soldiers out of men who turn tail at the first whiff of powder? The French had been right to snigger and to say that Italians were only good at stabbing in the back — and in the dark too.

Well, they'd make a better showing of it the next time, though he'd had to threaten to shoot any man who turned back from the bayonet charge. But they were still a rabble and the French still laughed at them behind their backs.

So he'd called in Anzani, who had finally licked them into shape. Little old Anzani, who never smiled or laughed, had worked the miracle which he, too easygoing by half, could never have achieved.

But the best joke of all was the uniform . . . those famous red shirts which they now all wore so proudly. A uniform, Anzani had insisted, they must have a uniform, otherwise they'll always remain a rabble. But all they would come up with were these overalls, which were going cheap because they couldn't be sent to Buenos Aires.

"At least they won't show the dirt!" the little man in the stores had joked. Dirt! Blood, he meant, but he didn't have the guts to say it.

And blood is what the legion had gone on spilling ever since — their own and others . . .

After his victory at Arroyo Grande, Oribe's advance on Montevideo was surprisingly leisurely. Probably he hoped that Montevideo would surrender without a fight, thus avoiding bloodshed. Instead, there was a change of government in the city and a new determination to hold out against the enemy. By the time Oribe reached Montevideo in mid-February 1843, defence preparations were well underway and the city was able to withstand a siege.

The most pressing need was to expand the defence force. Since at the time nearly half of the population of 30,000 were immigrants, it was inevitable that they should be called upon to play a major role in defence. Early in 1843, therefore, the French, Italian and Basque legions came into being.

The legionaries were all part-time volunteers. They received no pay, but both they and their families were given free rations. They were also promised substantial amounts of land and cattle when the war was over. Together with the large number of slaves freed for military service — a gesture which won the Uruguayans a good deal of credit in the eyes of the world — the legions made up the bulk of 'the army of the capital'.

In comparison with the 3000-strong French legion, the Italian legion, a mere 400 volunteers at the start, was very small indeed. Garibaldi was given overall responsibility for its organisation, but, as commander-in-chief of the navy, his main concern was to rebuild the fleet and so break the naval blockade on Montevideo. Over the next few months, however, he not only fought a number of small but successful engagements at sea but also kept a watchful eye on the newly-formed legion.

The legion's first experience of fighting ended in disgrace when two battalions ran away from battle. The soldiers' excuse was that they had no ammunition, but their rivals, the French, mocked them for it.

'I went red with shame when I heard of it,' Garibaldi records. There was only one way of wiping out this disgrace, he decided: the Italian legion must go into battle again and win a victory.

A week later, he led the legion into the attack himself, using what later became one of his favourite tactics: a bayonet charge. The manoeuvre was a success. The Italians redeemed themselves and shortly afterwards the legion was able to take its place alongside the French in a victory parade in the main square of Montevideo.

Gradually, through battles and raids like this, Garibaldi built up the morale and reputation of the legion. He brought in an old Italian revolutionary, Colonel Anzani, to supervise the training. Anzani, whom he had first met in Rio Grande, was a tough disciplinarian — unlike Garibaldi himself, who had a reputation for being lax.

The legion still had its setbacks. On one occasion the commander-in-chief, Colonel Mancini (whom Garibaldi himself had appointed) and his deputy decided to desert. Mancini was leading the legion in an attack on the enemy lines at the time and tried to persuade his men to desert with them. To the credit of the legion, however, only a few followed Mancini.

During the siege the legion also acquired the uniform for which they later became famous — their red shirts. But both the shirts and their colour were a matter of chance. The shirts were no more than overalls, destined for the butchers' yards of Buenos Aires but not delivered because of the war; and they had been dyed red to cover up the bloodstains from the animals.

In effect, the famous red shirts were a way of providing the volunteers with a cheap uniform — the overalls even had to be tied in at the waist so that the soldiers did not trip over in them — while the colour had no symbolic significance.

The legion was also given a flag — black with a volcano in the centre — which was more symbolic than the shirts. Black signified Italy in mourning — because she was not yet free; while the volcano was Vesuvius — waiting to erupt, like the revolution!

Even at this stage Garibaldi was probably looking forward to the day when the legion could be used in Italy — for which the present war was a useful training ground. Already his friend Cuneo, who brought out a paper in Italian in Montevideo, was publicising the achievements of the legion, often in an exaggerated form; while back in Europe Mazzini gave them wider circulation in England and Italy.

Thus Garibaldi's name was widely known long before he came back from South America. As one of his first biographers wrote, it was due to Mazzini and to Mazzini alone that Garibaldi's career in South America became so well known that when he returned to Europe in 1848 he was already a hero.

Garibaldi had also begun to develop his basic tactics for guerrilla warfare. He lacked the training and — perhaps the insight — to become a great strategist — a defect that showed up later when he sometimes had to command a full-sized army. But he had clear ideas about how to make the best use of untrained volunteers against regular soldiers.

Quick decisions were important, and so was the element of surprise in attack. He particularly stressed the need for courage because volunteer troops were liable to panic and needed to believe that they would win, even in the face of superior numbers. By the time he returned to Italy three years later, Garibaldi had developed a new kind of warfare out of his South American experiences which was virtually unknown in Europe.

Garibaldi's greatest achievement with the Italian legion was the battle of San Antonio in 1846. He had left Montevideo by sea the previous September with 700 soldiers, about half of whom were members of the legion. His small fleet was accompanied by the British and the French, who at this time were supporting the Uruguayan cause against Argentina. The allies first sailed up the River Plate, recapturing the Uruguayan city of Colonia and seizing the Argentine fortress on the island of Martín García.

Garibaldi then sailed up the River Uruguay and occupied a number of small towns on the way. There was a great outcry in Buenos Aires at the damage he inflicted, but this was precisely one of the objectives of the expedition. Some looting also took place, however, and this increased Garibaldi's reputation as a 'pirate'.

Finally, early in October, he reached his goal, the town of Salto, which was held by Colonel Lavalleja and a small force of about 700 soldiers. By occupying Salto, the Uruguayans hoped to regain some control over the north.

After defeating Lavalleja, Garibaldi fortified Salto and was able to withstand a siege by the notorious General Urquiza for nearly three weeks. Urquiza then gave up, leaving a small force to maintain the siege, which turned out to be ineffective.

The battle of San Antonio took place the following year, on February 8. Garibaldi got news that the main Uruguayan army, under General Medina, was approaching from the north and decided to go out to meet it with 150 soldiers of the legion and 100 Uruguayan cavalry. A short distance from the city he was attacked by a much larger force of Argentinian troops. He managed to take refuge in a ruined farmhouse, but at this point the cavalry left him and made off back to Salto.

All day the legionaries fought back against overwhelming odds. Garibaldi's dead and wounded piled up. Eventually, after fighting for over eight hours, he decided to retreat to Salto. Throughout the retreat he was pursued and harassed by the Argentinians, until Colonel Anzani, who had been left in charge of Salto and had heard what had happened, rode out to save him.

In the battle Garibaldi lost about forty men while another fifty of his troops were wounded. According to some reports, the Argentinians lost nearly five hundred troops. It was Garibaldi's proudest moment: the legion had at last proved its worth. 'I wouldn't exchange the honour of belonging to the legion for all the gold in the world!' he wrote in his report to Montevideo.

The legion had indeed come a long way since its members had broken ranks and fled during their first engagement.

9
The Hero

At night, long after the men had fallen quiet, he paced the deck, unable to sleep. At times like these he would have liked Anzani to keep him company, but he lay below, exhausted from coughing up his lungs, more than one foot in the grave, lucky if he made Europe.

"Stop worrying," Anzani had told him, in between bouts of coughing, holding his hand in a grip of steel. "You're a big man now — they wouldn't dare touch you even if they wanted to! And you've got the legion with you. Well, part of it," he added ruefully.

It was true: he'd made his name. Mazzini in England had seen to that, turning every little skirmish into a major battle and sending the good news all over Europe until everyone was talking of the Italian legion . . . and, if you please, **General** Garibaldi! The battle of San Antonio had clinched it for them.

Yet, when the day came to leave, they'd almost all stayed behind, making excuses that their life was there in America, but if the truth was known, just plain reluctant to face an uncertain future in Italy.

Not that he blamed them. For who really wanted them? Not the Pope, for all his liberal pretensions and protestations, nor the Grand Duke of Tuscany for another. He'd offered his sword to help in the struggle for liberty against the Austrians — but they hadn't responded.

He wasn't even sure of a pardon back in his own country — for something he'd done, or failed to do, a dozen years before!

Thank God it was a clear night, he thought, looking up at the stars. Their presence reassured him, as they often did at times like this. Almost as a matter of habit, he began to calculate the position of the ship.

"Slightly off course again!" he grumbled softly to himself and stumped off to have a word with the helmsman, worries about the future swallowed up by present concerns.

After the battle of San Antonio, Garibaldi was made a general, though he refused this honour at first, together with other rewards offered to the legion. 'Gifts and honours would weigh upon my soul,' he wrote back, 'because they have been bought with Italian blood.'

In the end he gave way to pressure, although he must have been aware that the praise he and the Italian legion were getting had caused resentment in Montevideo, where intense political squabbling was going on at the time.

He stayed on in Salto for several more months, where he was joined by Anita after the death of their favourite daughter, Rosita — 'the most beautiful, the sweetest of little girls'. Then, after a victory on the River Daiman, not far from Salto, he was recalled to Montevideo and was once more given a naval command. Over the next few months, he inflicted a great deal of damage on enemy shipping on the River Plate, even venturing as far as the Paraná itself.

Then, in 1847, things began to go wrong for the Uruguayans. They suffered military defeats in the north, and they also lost the support of the British for their cause. Both the British and the French were mainly concerned about their commercial interests in the River Plate and had tried more than once to bring about an end to the war. Rosas had now been persuaded to accept the peace proposals and there was strong support for these in certain quarters of Montevideo, where many were tired of the long siege.

In the end, however, the war party won the day. Garibaldi too had come out against the peace proposals, mainly because the British wanted to dissolve the legions, which they saw as an obstacle to peace. He refused point-blank to disband the Italian legion, for which he had other plans. The British respected his integrity but, in the end, withdrew their support for the Uruguayans, who now had to struggle on on their own, with some assistance from the French.

For some time Garibaldi's thoughts had been turning to Italy. Even while he was in Salto in 1846, he had written to Cuneo asking him to try to arrange a passage to Nice for Anita and his family. 'We haven't got any money, though!' he had warned him. The moment to leave had now come. He had a reputation back home and even a small fighting force to offer. All he needed was an opportunity to fight for Italy — and some reasonable guarantee that he would not be arrested for treason.

In Italy the situation was very encouraging. In 1846 a new pope, Pius IX, had introduced some liberal reforms, even releasing a number of political prisoners and although he was far less liberal in his outlook than he appeared to be at the time, for a short while the new pope became a popular figure.

Even the rulers of other states — Naples, Tuscany and Sardinia —

33

had been forced to follow his example and to bring in some constitutional reforms too. None of these, however, went very deep, and much more needed to be done before the people could be said to be 'free'. Besides, there were still the Austrians, who ruled over Lombardy and Venice, and indirectly controlled other states as well.

In his enthusiasm for a role to help shape a new Italy, perhaps by driving out the Austrians, Garibaldi had written to the Pope, offering the support of the Italian legion. But he got no reply. He also wrote to the Grand Duke of Tuscany, offering his services, and for a different reason to Charles Albert, the King of Sardinia, asking for a pardon.

But, in spite of this lack of response, Garibaldi was still determined to go back to Italy and he decided to send Anita on ahead — perhaps as a way of testing reaction to his own return.

Anita left Montevideo in January 1848, taking with her their three children. In addition to Menotti, they now had a daughter, Teresita, born in 1845, and a son, Ricciotti, born in 1847 and named after another Italian martyr, Nicola Ricciotti. When she arrived in Nice, to stay with Garibaldi's mother, Anita was greeted by huge crowds, flags and cries of "Long live Garibaldi! Long live the family of our Garibaldi!"

Even so, Garibaldi himself could not be sure that it would be safe for him to return to Piedmont, and his plan was to land on the coast of Tuscany and perhaps to start some kind of revolution there. A member of 'Young Italy', Giacomo Medici, had already been sent on ahead to prepare the way.

Garibaldi himself finally left Montevideo on April 15. Sufficient money had been raised to hire or buy a ship, the *Bifronte*, which left Montevideo flying the Italian flag. By the time it reached Italy, however, it had been rechristened *La Speranza* (Hope!) and was, for safety's sake, flying the flag of Uruguay.

In the end only a small number of the legion — between sixty and seventy — actually left with Garibaldi, and these were mostly soldiers who had fought with him at San Antonio. The number perhaps was disappointing, but the prospects for their return did not look promising.

The *Bifronte* slipped away quietly from Montevideo. There were no ceremonies to send the legion on its way. Perhaps the authorities did not want to make too much of the fact that they were losing their most distinguished fighter, although they had given him permission to take a ship and some arms as well — two cannons and some muskets.

Garibaldi left Montevideo as he had lived there throughout: a poor man who sometimes could not afford to buy candles for his family and who rarely had more than one change of shirt. The only thing he took with him were the bones of his daughter Rosita, which, to keep a promise he had made to Anita, he had secretly removed from the cemetery in Montevideo.

The voyage back to Europe took sixty-eight days. There was training on board for the legionaries — exercises to keep their bodies fit and education classes to prepare their minds. In the evening they sat on deck and sang patriotic songs. From time to time, though, Garibaldi must have wondered what would happen when they landed in Tuscany. Was it just another mad escapade?

What no one on board the *Speranza* knew, because they had sailed just before the news reached Montevideo, was that revolution had broken out all over Europe. The first they heard about it was when the captain of the ship went ashore to buy some food at Alicante, soon after they had passed through the Straits of Gibraltar. The news sent him rushing back to the ship.

There had been revolutions in Paris and Vienna! All over Italy there had been uprisings in a hundred cities — from Palermo in the south to Milan and Venice in the north! The Austrians were on the run! They could not have chosen a better time to return to Europe and when Garibaldi heard the news, he realised that a change of plan was needed. He decided to head straight for Nice.

10
The Guerrilla Fighter

He tossed and turned on the hard bed and cursed the fever that had tormented and weakened him these past weeks.

And he cursed even more the king who had betrayed them all through his hesitation and lack of resolution. Well, history would judge him!

Yes, though he had read weakness in the man's eyes, he had been ready to trust him and to offer his sword in his service. For the sake of Italy he had been prepared to set aside his republican principles and to become, for a time at any rate, a monarchist.

And for this he had been reviled. Mazzini had spoken against him and Medici too. And they had got at the one he loved most, old Anzani, who with his dying breath had begged him not to betray the cause of the people.

Him! Betray the people! That hurt, and would go on hurting, because Anzani, dead now, would never know the truth.

And then (what irony!) the king hadn't wanted him and he was lucky to be allowed to fight at all! All his experience nearly wasted!

Still, in the end he'd shown them. Mazzini had slipped away, not man enough to carry on the fight, while he had gone on battling for the cause, almost single-handed, with just a handful of men, long after the rest had swallowed the king's shameful peace.

And he could have gone on fighting still, but for this illness, which only rest could put right . . . and the warmth of Anita's nursing.

There had been a good deal to celebrate during that short voyage along the coast to Nice.

Venice had expelled the Austrians and had set up a republic under Daniele Manin. The Austrians had been driven out of Milan after five days of fierce and bloody fighting in the streets. Charles Albert, King of Sardinia, had declared war on Austria and had marched into Lombardy to support the Milanese.

Although Charles was not a man to inspire confidence — as a young officer he had betrayed the revolution of 1821 and had later become a repressive ruler himself — Italians from all over Italy were coming north in their thousands to fight under his leadership.

Pope Pius, on the other hand, had refused to join in against the Austrians, having little enthusiasm for the cause of Italian unity, and for this his popularity immediately suffered.

It was in this atmosphere of intense excitement, a feeling that Italy was at last about to be free and united, that Garibaldi arrived in Nice on June 21 1848. He had already decided to offer his services to the king who, fourteen years before, had sentenced him to death.

At Nice he met with a reception similar to the one given to Anita, who was there to greet him at the harbour. There were banquets and speech-making and Garibaldi spoke warmly of the king's role. He had barely time to see his mother, his wife and family before he was off to the war, taking with him over one hundred new volunteers.

Passing through Genoa, where there were more celebrations in his honour, he spent some time with Anzani, who now had only a few days to live. There was some concern, especially among the members of 'Young Italy', that Garibaldi was being too enthusiastic about the king, who, many thought, was mainly interested in expanding his own kingdom. Anzani believed in Garibaldi — the future of Italy lies in his hands, he is alleged to have told Medici — but reminded him that he must be careful not to betray the people.

The king, with an army of nearly 100,000 under his command, was not impressed with Garibaldi's offer of a mere 200 volunteers, many untrained, and with his request to be made a general.

Charles Albert, his advisers and the military, most of whom had little experience of actual warfare, did not want 'the man from Montevideo' around their headquarters at Mantua. Garibaldi was sent off to Turin, on the pretext that something might be found for him there. In reality, they wanted him out of the way as quickly as possible.

In Turin, it was suggested that he might like to go to Venice, to help Manin as a kind of 'corsaro', which was how he was viewed. The idea did not appeal to Garibaldi, who moved on to Milan. There he was received in great style and was made a general.

But the famous red shirts — which all the volunteers were longing to wear — did not meet with approval. It was pointed out, perhaps rightly, that they made the men easy targets.

"But we must have uniforms," protested Garibaldi. It was not the first time he had come up against this problem.

The official response was to issue them with some old Austrian uniforms. The volunteers were not pleased, but they managed to convert the white jackets into some sort of blouse — though it made them look like 'a regiment of cooks', according to Medici.

At Bergamo, where he had been sent to train volunteer troops, Garibaldi got the bad news that Charles Albert had been defeated at Custoza on July 24 and was now in full retreat towards Milan, pursued by the Austrian commander, Marshal Radetzky. Garibaldi was ordered to move to Monza and to try to delay an attack on Milan itself.

At Monza there was further bad news: the king was trying to negotiate an armistice and meanwhile, to save the civilian population, had evacuated Milan. Many of Garibaldi's volunteers chose this moment to desert.

"What they do there has nothing to do with us," Garibaldi told his troops. "The Italian war against Austria will go on!" He then marched towards Como, intending to carry on fighting a guerrilla war.

He had been joined at Monza by Mazzini and Medici, who brought with them more volunteers. For a time Mazzini even served under Garibaldi, continuing to write articles for his paper, which he proudly signed as 'Giuseppe Mazzini, a soldier of Garibaldi's legion'.

But a certain coldness had developed between the two men. Mazzini had disapproved of Garibaldi's enthusiasm for the king and events had proved him right. On his side, Garibaldi criticised Mazzini for retreating to Switzerland shortly afterwards.

From Como, Garibaldi marched west, through Varese, as far as Castelleto Ticino, near Lago Maggiore. Here there was more depressing news: Radetzky had occupied Milan and Charles Albert had signed an armistice. Only Venice was still managing to hold out.

Garibaldi himself was ordered to disband his volunteers.

His response was to try to increase his small army of 400 by rounding up deserters. He also issued a declaration, denouncing Charles Albert as a traitor.

'The King of Sardinia may wish to keep his throne by guile and cowardice — but I and my companions do not want to save our lives in this disgraceful way!'

Garibaldi must have known that he could not win in the end, but perhaps he hoped that his example would encourage the peasants to rise against the Austrians. He had yet to learn that they had little interest in the fight for Italian unity.

For almost two weeks Garibaldi waged a private war against the Austrians. He first led his volunteers, who now numbered about seven hundred and fifty, towards Arona on Lago Maggiore, where he seized two paddle-steamers and crossed over to Luino on the eastern bank. There he had his first engagement with the Austrians. He managed to beat off their attack and even took some prisoners. It was a small but decisive victory, and showed the Austrians that he could not be ignored.

He noticed, however, that the inhabitants of Luino did not rush to help him, preferring to watch the battle as if it were a kind of theatrical performance. Both here and elsewhere he found the peasants unco-operative, ready even to help the Austrians if they were paid for it. And everywhere he went there was the problem of getting food for his men.

Finally, on August 26, Garibaldi reached Morazzone, a small hill town south of Varese. The Austrians attacked almost at once. He managed to hold out throughout the day, while the Austrians bombarded and even tried to set fire to the town. Then, under cover of darkness, he slipped away with as many men as wanted to follow him.

By now he realised that it was hopeless to try to continue the fight against the Austrians. He decided, therefore, to disband his volunteers — who now numbered only about seventy — and told them to make their own way home via Switzerland.

He himself slipped across the frontier to Lugano, where he collapsed, completely exhausted, in an inn. He was suffering from a fever which had dogged him throughout the campaign.

There in the inn he was later found by Medici, to whom he outlined his plans for continuing the struggle. According to Garibaldi, Medici, who was a devoted follower of Mazzini, was contemptuous.

"We are going to do better than that!" he sneered.

Garibaldi was deeply discouraged. He had fought a hard campaign and now, it seemed, Mazzini and Medici were planning something behind his back. He decided, therefore, to return to Nice, to see his family and to try to recover from his illness.

11
The Revolutionary

Rossi dead . . . and the Pope gone! The news sent a shock wave through him, part fear, part pleasure.

He didn't, couldn't approve of murder. Assassination was a crime. It must be, because taking a man's life was wrong. In war, of course, men were killed all the time. Striking a man down in cold blood was different, though.

But the Pope gone . . . who had posed as a reformer and had deluded them all . . . who had betrayed them in their struggle against the Austrians.

Surely, sometimes, the end justified the means?

The Pope gone . . . Suddenly there was hope where there had been none. Rome was free, no longer a priest-ridden city. Rome could resume her rightful place as the capital of Italy. His adolescent dream of twenty years past was being fulfilled!

Surely that excused the assassin's dagger, justified the loss of one man's life?

The Pope gone . . . But that would not be the end of it. There would be trouble for this, of course. From his place of exile he would summon up his hounds to protect him . . . Naples, Spain, Austria. They would gather, snapping and snarling, outside the walls of Rome, savage in the service of their master.

No time to be wasted, then. Venice — a lost cause if ever there was — would have to do without him. Rome had greater need of him, and there he must go — quickly!

For the moment the struggle against the Austrians was over. The enemy was still there, in Italy, but through his example Garibaldi had inspired Italians throughout the peninsula and had shown that their powerful adversary was not invincible.

He had impressed the Austrians too, which was why Radetzky had ordered him to be hunted down. Years later, the man who had been sent to do this, General d'Aspre, told a Piedmontese official: "You turned your backs on the one man who could have helped you win your war — Garibaldi!"

For three weeks Garibaldi stayed in Nice, recovering his health and enjoying the company of his family, whom he had scarcely seen. But he was disappointed and restless — 'more sick in spirit than in body' he said of himself in his memoirs — and above all anxious to carry on the fight.

On a visit to Genoa, he was pressed to go to Sicily, where there had been an uprising against the Bourbon ruler, the King of Naples. It was the opportunity he had been looking for and on October 24 1848 he embarked with seventy-two volunteers on a French ship bound for Palermo, together with Anita, who had seen little of her husband that year and was ready to fight at his side, as in the old days.

Garibaldi got no further than Livorno, a few miles down the coast, where he was greeted by enthusiastic crowds. Two months before there had been a revolution here, which had obliged the Duke of Tuscany to appoint a radical government in Florence, the capital.

The revolutionaries were anxious to keep Garibaldi with them. Why must he go to Sicily? He could become the commander of the Tuscan army and attack the King of Naples on the mainland! Garibaldi liked the idea — especially, perhaps, the chance of a real military command. Telegrams were exchanged between Livorno and the capital. The replies of the government were evasive . . . but the ship sailed for Palermo without Garibaldi and his men.

The telegrams between Livorno and Florence continued. It was becoming clear, however, that the government, though radical, was reluctant to offer him the command he wanted. Probably it was felt that a direct attack on the King of Naples was too risky and might also provoke the Austrians.

In the end it was suggested that instead Garibaldi might like to go to help Manin in Venice. With his experience of beating naval blockades in South America he could provide the city with just the kind of support it needed.

This time Garibaldi seems to have been taken with the idea, especially when the government offered to provide his 350 volunteers with uniforms and arms. On November 3 he left by train for Florence, where he was enthusiastically received by the crowds. Garibaldi, perhaps, began to get carried away. Addressing a huge audience in a theatre, he attacked the government in violent terms:

"The Tuscan government should be forced and whipped along — by demonstrations, that is! Italy can choose one of two ways with her rulers. She can either overthrow them or drag them along with her. There is no middle way!"

No middle way! His audience was delighted; but not the government. Their offer of uniforms and guns was withdrawn. His rations were cut off and Garibaldi and his 'plague of locusts' were invited to be on their way to Venice as soon as possible.

Winter had come early and snow lay knee-deep on the mountain roads across the Apennines. Few of the volunteers had proper clothing or boots, and some were in rags. When they reached the pass, they were stopped by a detachment of Swiss guards. Their route now took them through Romagna, one of the Papal States, and the guards had been ordered to bar their way.

Garibaldi went into Bologna alone to sort out the problem with the Pope's military commander. There he met with yet another enthusiastic welcome and the crowds even insisted on pulling his carriage through the streets. In the end, permission was given to proceed to Ravenna, his last stop before Venice.

He reached Ravenna on November 16, and then proposed to wait for some volunteers from Mantua before going on. At least, this was the reason he gave for delaying. It is possible he had begun to have doubts about going to Venice, where the situation was critical. The authorities ordered him to leave, even threatening to disarm him. Garibaldi threatened to fight back . . . and still went on delaying.

Then came some news that made him change his plans completely.

After Pope Pius IX had refused to support the war against Austria, the reaction against him had gone on gathering strength. In Rome itself the radical movement, led by the journalist Pietro Sterbini and a militant wine merchant from Trastevere, Angelo Brunetti — better known as Ciceruacchio — had grown so powerful that Pius was forced to appoint a new prime minister. He chose Count Pellegrini Rossi.

Rossi was moderately liberal in outlook — much the same as the Pope himself when he was first elected. But to the radicals he seemed very conservative. And Rossi had no doubt that law and order could — and would — be restored.

On November 15, as he left his carriage to attend a meeting of parliament, he found himself surrounded by a hostile crowd of demonstrators. He was a proud, contemptuous man and pretended to ignore the shouts of 'Death to Rossi! Death to Rossi!' The crowd pressed closer, completely surrounding him. First one blow was struck, then another. Fifty blows were struck in all . . . and Rossi lay dead.

The Pope quickly formed a new and radical government, which included even Sterbini. But he soon realised that it was too late to hold back the revolution. On November 24 he fled, disguised as an ordinary priest, and took refuge at Gaeta with the King of Naples.

12
The Defender of Rome (1)

He was sad to see Anita leave, but how could he take her with him to Rome, that indefensible city that must, all the same, be defended? Maybe he'd succeed, who knows, but they'd wasted time and there was no making up for that.

For weeks, months now, he'd argued with them, trying to make them see sense. But all he'd got was promises and still more promises. They were all the same, these politicians, right or left, royalist or republican. All they wanted to do was to make speeches, like actors on a stage, wondering all the while what impression they were making.

And all the time he was crying out for men. Not 500 but 5000, because it took time to train them. And men needed boots and overcoats. They needed rations. And above all they needed arms.

But they'd starved him of muskets and in the end he'd had to make do with pikes and lances knocked up by the local blacksmiths of Rieti. Better than nothing, perhaps, but what match would they be against professionals?

Well, now the fat was in the fire. The Pope had got his avengers — the French of all people, ordered against them by the nephew of the man who'd nearly made Italy into a nation. They were knocking at the gates, asking ever so politely: "Please let us in . . . or else!"

And so they'd sent for Garibaldi — the man who looked like Christ and could therefore work miracles!

For that was what was going to be needed!

As soon as he heard that Rome was in the hands of the revolutionaries, Garibaldi left his volunteers at nearby Cesena and hurried south.

But the republicans were in no hurry to let his troops into the city — it had even been suggested they might frighten the ladies! — nor to encourage him to recruit more men. For the moment he was allowed 500 troops and no more. He himself was given the rank of colonel but was asked to remain in the north.

It was not exactly the treatment he had expected!

He spent the winter at Macerata, from where he was elected to the new assembly, with the help of votes cast by his own troops. After that he moved south to Rieti, where he was once more joined by Anita.

In due course he was allowed to increase the number of his troops to 1000, but he was soon maintaining a larger number, about 1300, out of the money he was given. Few weapons were provided but Garibaldi arranged for his men to be equipped with home-made lances. He was determined to be ready when the call eventually came.

Early in February Garibaldi went to Rome himself to take his seat in the new assembly. He was suffering from a severe attack of arthritis at the time and had to be carried into the chamber. It was an important occasion and the republicans perhaps felt that they were on stage. Things had to be done formally, with ceremony and speeches.

Garibaldi too recognised that it was an important occasion: a republic had to be declared. They owed that much to the people and he told them so, bluntly. The deputies applauded, but the speechmaking went on for four more days.

Occasions such as this increased Garibaldi's growing distrust of politicians.

But at least Mazzini was sent for without debate. He was given a key role and quickly established himself as a man of action and as the leader of the Triumvirate, the three men appointed to govern Rome. From Rieti, Garibaldi, who earlier had been critical of Mazzini, sent his greetings. 'Don't forget,' he wrote, 'that here in Rieti you can still find your friends in the faith — and they haven't changed.'

The date was April 3 1849 — and Garibaldi was still waiting to be called to Rome and given a command.

Meanwhile the Pope had lost no time in calling upon all Catholic countries to restore him. Ferdinand of Naples, with whom he had taken refuge, had advanced towards Rome with his army — but then hesitated. Spain sent a small contingent to help. Austria too was eager to intervene.

Then on March 20 Charles Albert, still smarting from his defeat at Custoza the previous summer, broke the armistice and once more marched into Lombardy. Only nine days later he was defeated at Novara by Marshal Radetzky and was forced to abdicate in favour of his son, who came to the throne as Victor Emmanuel II. Radetzky then wanted to march south to help the Pope, but the French made it clear that Austria was not to interfere.

Of all the Catholic countries, liberal republican France had responded most decisively to the Pope's appeal. Louis Napoleon, nephew of Napoleon Bonaparte, had recently been elected president of the Second Republic and under pressure from the Catholic majority — whose support he needed for the coup he was then preparing — agreed to act against the newly-declared republic.

Marshal Oudinot was despatched with a force of 9000 men, although the exact purpose of his mission was kept secret, even from his own troops. Oudinot was a conservative and a devout Catholic and there was no doubt in his own mind what he intended to do: throw out the republicans and restore the Pope.

On April 25 he disembarked at Civitavecchia, only fifty miles north of Rome. But he still professed that his main purpose was to support the new republic against the Austrians — though the Pope would have to be taken back too. A senior officer was despatched to give this message to the republicans.

"But what if the people do not want the Pope restored?" Mazzini asked the French envoy.

"He will be restored all the same," he was told.

Back in the assembly Mazzini presented the stark alternatives to his colleagues. "We have two courses of action," he said. "We can let the French in . . . or we can resist — resist to the bitter end." The matter was debated, but the assembly had no doubts about what they proposed to do: they were going to resist.

The French envoy was told to take that message back to Marshal Oudinot.

Preparations for the defence of the city were immediately put underway and, almost overnight, the Romans, who under the Pope had been almost ungovernable, proved themselves to be model citizens. Street defences were organised in case the French got into the city. Medical services were set up and several churches were converted into hospitals. Personal weapons of all kinds were pooled and crime virtually disappeared.

All this was reported back to the French. But Marshal Oudinot had such a poor opinion of the Italians that he still refused to believe that the republicans would fight.

The republican forces were put under General Avezzana, a hardened revolutionary fighter who had returned from exile in America. Altogether he had an army of about 20,000 men, but the bulk of these were guarding the frontiers against the Austrians and the Neapolitans. Avezzana at once sent for Garibaldi and put him in charge of one of the four brigades into which the defence forces were divided.

As an experienced fighter, Garibaldi quickly appreciated that the Villa Corsini and other buildings on the piece of high ground just outside the walls on the western side must not be allowed to fall into the hands of the French, otherwise they would be in a position to dominate the city. He got permission to occupy these and so, when the French reached Rome on April 30 and approached the walls in the area of the Vatican, he was able to bombard them from above.

Cannons were fired as the French approached the city. But Oudinot still did not believe that the Italians would resist until his men began to fall under a hail of cannon and musket shot from the walls. The French commanders were then forced to regroup in order to make fresh plans for the assault on the city.

Garibaldi chose this moment to send in the first of his troops, a detachment of 300 students, all virtually untrained. These were soon driven back by the French regulars, even though he had also sent in some of his own legion in support. He then sent in a much larger force and himself led the counter-attack.

In the fierce fighting that followed, Garibaldi was wounded, though he concealed this until after the battle. Eventually the French were forced to retreat, leaving behind about 500 dead and wounded, and 365 prisoners.

There were great celebrations in Rome that night. The city was ablaze with lights and there was singing and dancing in the streets. The French prisoners were given cigars and drinks and taken on a tour of the city. A few days later they were released and sent back to rejoin Marshal Oudinot. The republicans hoped that the French would be appeased and would give up their idea of occupying Rome.

Instead Louis Napoleon was affronted: French pride had been wounded and must be avenged. He at once arranged to send reinforcements. He needed to ingratiate himself with the Catholics before seizing power and crowning himself emperor.

Meanwhile, on May 1, the King of Naples invaded republican territory with 10,000 troops and a few days later Garibaldi was sent out to meet this new threat with his volunteers. After a good deal of reconnaissance, he decided to wait for the Neapolitans to attack and settled his own men on a small hill near the village of Palestrina.

When the Neapolitans attacked on May 9, he used one of his favourite tactics of holding fire until the very last moment and then following this up with a bayonet charge. On this occasion he was able to complete the rout of the Neapolitans by sending in some cavalry which had been attached to him.

Almost immediately Garibaldi was recalled to Rome to defend the city against possible attack. His return proved unnecessary, however, because Ferdinand de Lesseps (later famous as the engineer responsible for building the Suez Canal) had been sent to negotiate an armistice with the republicans — thus giving Oudinot time to wait for his reinforcements and Louis Napoleon for his majority in the new French assembly.

Garibaldi was again sent out against the Neapolitans, but this time as part of a much larger army, under General Roselli, who had replaced Avezzana as commander-in-chief of the defence forces. Roselli was a professional soldier, but with little experience of actual warfare and inclined to be rather cautious. He had, however, planned his campaign against the retreating Neapolitan forces carefully and he now had difficulty in preventing it from being upset by the impatient Garibaldi, who was continually rushing ahead of the main body of the army.

On May 19 Garibaldi, whose instructions were only to reconnoitre but not to engage the enemy, found himself involved in a skirmish with the enemy near Velletri and narrowly escaped with his life when he tried to prevent his cavalry from retreating. In the engagement he lost at least 100 dead and wounded. The Neapolitans continued their retreat; Garibaldi wanted to pursue them across the border into their own territory and had to be held back by Roselli. There was increasing friction between the two men and Garibaldi did not attempt to conceal his contempt for Roselli as a commander.

There was friction between Garibaldi and Mazzini too over the defence of Rome, which Garibaldi felt should be in his hands. He believed, perhaps rightly, that in the end Rome would prove indefensible and that the republic could only survive if a guerrilla war was carried on from the mountains around Rome.

Mazzini, while he too had his own doubts about the survival of the republic, thought that Rome had to be defended to the last: it was the symbol of the revolutionary struggle.

Both men clung to their own beliefs to the end.

At this point Garibaldi was recalled to Rome, together with the rest of the republican forces. The threat of an Austrian attack from the north seemed to be growing every day. As things turned out, however, the real and immediate danger lay not from the Austrians but from the French, who were encamped not far from the city on the pretext of defending it from attack.

13
The Defender of Rome (2)

Dawn was breaking and they were beginning to stir in the French camp. Soon some French sharpshooter would be taking a crack at him, hoping to be the one who could boast he'd downed the general as he lit his first cigar of the day!

Well, he'd keep them waiting for a bit! He needed a few more moments of silence for reflection.

He was past the point of anger, and all the resentment against Mazzini and those other speechmakers had long since drained out of him. No point in raging. The worst had already happened. They had lost the Corsini and nothing short of a miracle could save them.

He knew it and they knew it — the politicians who never stopped talking and the generals who made mistakes and the men who died for those mistakes and the women who wept over their men who had died while their children chased after cannon-balls, hoping to earn a few pence.

The glory-light shone in their eyes, for there was little left except glory and of course death. They were playing out the last act of this heroic drama and half Europe was in the wings.

They would be remembered long after the curtain had gone down.

And was the curtain coming down for him too, he wondered? He hoped death, if it did come, would be quick.

And that reminded him: he was keeping the marksmen waiting! He lit his cigar and smiled as the first flakes of masonry from the wall behind him began to flutter like petals to the ground around him.

On May 31 1849 de Lesseps finally concluded a treaty with the republicans, in which it was agreed that the French would remain near Rome but would not attempt to enter the city.

Pleased with his success, de Lesseps hurried back to report this to Marshal Oudinot. To his astonishment, Oudinot announced that he was ignoring the treaty: his instructions from Paris were to end the armistice and enter Rome.

It was no less than the truth, as de Lesseps later found out for himself when he got back to Paris, disgraced for having carried out his instructions. Louis Napoleon had by this time secured his majority in the assembly and could now go ahead with his plans to restore the Pope.

Oudinot soon made it clear to the republicans that he did not feel bound by the treaty. Roselli had asked for the armistice to be extended indefinitely; otherwise, he pointed out, he would not be able to deal with the rapidly approaching Austrian army.

Oudinot's reply was blunt, and also in part ambiguous: 'The orders of my government . . . require me to enter Rome as soon as possible. However,' he concluded, 'I will put off attacking the place until Monday morning.' This was to give foreign residents time to leave the city if they so wanted. Monday morning was June 4.

In desperation Mazzini sent a note to Garibaldi, who, on his return from Velletri had retired to bed, suffering from a wound, from bruises and from another attack of arthritis.

What should they do about the defence of Rome in the face of this new threat, Mazzini asked. The matter was especially serious because the French now had over 20,000 troops.

'I can only exist for the good of the republic in one of two ways,' Garibaldi replied. 'As a dictator with unlimited powers or as a simple soldier. Choose!'

Garibaldi did not want power for himself, but he believed that in times of crisis only a strong man could save the state.

Mazzini ignored Garibaldi's unacceptable alternatives and once again asked for his advice. Put Avezzana in charge of the defence, he was told. If he himself was called on to defend Rome, he would do so — but as 'a simple soldier of the Italian legion'.

It was as much as Mazzini could get out of Garibaldi at this stage.

It had been assumed from Oudinot's letter that no attack would take place until Monday morning. But then, on June 2, twenty-four hours after the armistice had expired, French troops moved forward and occupied the Villa Corsini and Pamfili, just outside Porta San Pancrazio. The 'place' referred to in Oudinot's letter meant strictly the city of Rome; it did not include areas *outside* the walls.

And the Villa Corsini stood precisely on the high ground which, before the first attack, Garibaldi had stressed was so vital to the defence of the city. During the armistice it had been only lightly guarded and the French met with little resistance.

Garibaldi hurried to the scene of battle as soon as the news was brought to him, all thoughts of serving as 'a simple soldier' set aside. The Villa Corsini had to be recaptured at all costs, he decided, otherwise Rome was lost. Roselli put him in charge of the operation, with 6000 troops at his command.

The battle for the Villa Corsini lasted all the following day and into the night. From the Roman side, the villa could only be approached through a long narrow lane, which was completely covered by French fire. Garibaldi made attack after attack up this narrow path, but only sending in a small number of troops each time, without proper covering fire . . . and always with the same fatal result.

At the end of the day he had lost 1000 dead or wounded and, in spite of countless acts of heroism by the republicans, the Villa Corsini and the high ground overlooking the city walls remained firmly in French hands.

Oudinot was now able to put Rome under siege.

The republicans held out against the French for a whole month, constantly bombarded by the artillery at the Villa Corsini. The city was being slowly destroyed. At one point the situation was so desperate that Mazzini wanted to try to recapture the villa by means of a mass attack, using the entire army supported by volunteers from the people.

It was Garibaldi — who had earlier begged to be allowed to attack first the French and then the Neapolitans — who now advised defence.

His headquarters in the Villa Savorelli were a favourite target of the French artillery and Garibaldi himself used to present himself at dawn every day on the balcony of the villa, just to provide some practice for the French marksmen.

At other times during the day, a conspicuous figure in a white poncho, usually smoking a cigar, he could be seen riding around on a tour of inspection, inspiring everyone with confidence. His handling of the attack on the Villa Corsini had been criticised, but he remained as popular as ever.

Meanwhile Oudinot was slowly moving closer to the city walls and to Porta San Pancrazio, getting ready for an assault by digging trenches that led towards the city. Garibaldi harassed the French operations as much as possible, but the work went on.

The assault came on the night of June 21 and after fierce fighting the defence forces were driven back, leaving the French in command of three points south of Porta San Pancrazio. Garibaldi withdrew his troops behind the Aurelian Wall and moved his headquarters to the Villa Spada. The Villa Savorelli had by now been reduced to a heap of rubble by the French artillery.

On June 26 he was joined once more by Anita, sent back to Nice when he left Rieti. She had come against her husband's wishes, for she was now several months pregnant. All the same, he was delighted to see her, and proud too, because she had once again risked her life to be at his side.

Only a few days before, he had written her a letter, not knowing that she was already on her way and would never, as it turned out, read what he had written. In it he describes some of the daily events of the siege:

'The French friars of Cardinal Oudinot (these were their nicknames for the general and his men) amuse themselves by bombarding us with cannon-balls, but we are much too used to it to bother. Here the women and children run after the balls and practically fight to get hold of them.

'These people are worthy of their past greatness. Here they live, die and suffer loss of limb, all to the cry of *"Viva la Repubblica!"* One hour of our life in Rome is worth a century of ordinary existence . . .'

Yet only two months before he had remarked in a letter to Anita that he was 'ashamed to belong to a family which has so many cowards.'

On June 29, just three days after Anita's arrival, the French began their final attack on the city. It was St Peter's day, a traditional Roman holiday which the people decided to celebrate with the usual festivities, with dancing and bonfires in the streets, to show their defiance of the French.

Oudinot had planned the attack for midnight but there was a violent thunderstorm and he had to wait until 2.00 am. Then the cannons began by battering down the Roman defence of the Janiculum and he was able to send in his infantry.

His soldiers had been instructed to take no prisoners. Resistance was stubborn and the fierce hand-to-hand fighting went on all day. By the afternoon, however, the French had driven back the republicans and had taken possession of the Janiculum and the Aurelian Wall. The end was near.

Garibaldi, who had been in the thick of the fighting all day, was summoned to the assembly. He arrived, his shirt stained with blood and his sword bent, and was greeted with a cheer. Various proposals were presented and discussed at length. Many deputies wanted simply to capitulate, to avoid further bloodshed and destruction. Mazzini wanted to defend Rome street by street, from behind the barricades, in true revolutionary style. When asked his opinion, Garibaldi proposed that they should take to the hills and carry on the fight from there.

'Wherever we are, there Rome will be!' he declared.

The debate went on and on and Oudinot granted them an armistice in order to reach a decision. In the end, it was decided to surrender. The resolution of the assembly read: 'The Roman Assembly ceases from a defence which has become impossible and remains at its place.'

The republic was finished. But, as a final gesture, Garibaldi was — at last — made commander-in-chief and was given permission to leave Rome with as many soldiers as would follow him. Mazzini and his two colleagues formally resigned. He was given a foreign passport, like many others of the revolutionaries, and eventually escaped to England.

Garibaldi too was also offered a passport by the Americans but declined. He had other plans.

At five o'clock on the afternoon of July 2 he appeared on horseback in St Peter's Square, which was filled with soldiers. He held up his hand for silence.

"I am leaving Rome," he told the crowd. "Whoever wishes to continue the war, come with me. I cannot offer you pay or food or even anywhere to sleep at night. All I can offer is hunger and cold, forced marches, battles and in the end perhaps . . . death. But if you love your country in your heart and not just in word alone, follow me!"

Two hours later about 4000 men assembled near the Lateran Gate and marched out of Rome. Garibaldi was at their head and Anita, disguised as a man and with her hair cut short, rode at her husband's side.

14
The Fugitive

So far, so good, he reflected, as he squatted on the hillside and scoured the countryside below for any sign of Oudinot's troops. His ruse had worked. For the moment at least he'd given them the slip.

How peaceful the countryside looked that evening . . . the peasants returning home from their day's labour in the fields, unaware of war, uninterested perhaps in the struggle that had taken place in Rome only a few miles away. There was a smell of woodsmoke in the air, reminding him that he had not eaten all day.

And somewhere in the vineyards below a boy had begun to sing, much as he himself used to sing as he walked the hills behind Nice.

Yet this boy's song, plaintive, melancholy, was different. It was the bitter fruit of centuries of deprivation and oppression, which would continue so long as the people were without power and the Church and alien rulers controlled their lives.

His eye turned towards Rome, where the dome of St Peter's was bathed in the evening light. The French were the masters of the city now. With their help the Church had clawed its way back to power.

Take it all in, he told himself, and fix it firmly in your mind's eye, for you may never see Rome again! He had got 4000 men safely out of the city, but already some were slipping away and he hadn't the heart to blame them. They had seen the chance to get clear by clinging to his coat-tails, to get back to their families.

Only fools would want to haul wagons and cannon over mountain passes and along unmade roads! Only fools would dream they could escape the clutches of three armies in hot pursuit — and a fourth waiting for them across the frontier in Tuscany! Only fools would want to go and fight in Venice, its defences already crumbling . . .

The light was fading and Anita was calling him. He got to his feet, painfully, cursing the stiffness that was always in his bones these days. He remembered it was his birthday — he was forty-two! This time last year he was on his way to offer his services to the king!

It was dark now in the plain below and the boy's song had ended.

The French entered Rome on July 3 to find that their chief prize had escaped them. But perhaps they were not unduly concerned. Against Garibaldi's force of 4000 men, Oudinot was able to send in pursuit a combined army of over 20,000 French, Spanish and Neapolitan troops, while in the north, in Tuscany and Romagna, the Austrians were waiting for him with almost the same number. There could be little doubt in their minds that Garibaldi would soon be captured.

Garibaldi's immediate concern was to throw the French off his trail. He headed first for Tivoli, due east of Rome, and then started off towards the south, to give the impression that he was making for the Kingdom of Naples. Almost immediately, however, he turned north, through Monte Rotondo, reaching Terni on July 8, where he was joined by an eccentric Englishman, Colonel Forbes, with 700 soldiers. He then continued north to Todi, which he reached on July 11.

But pursuit was only one of the problems that Garbaldi had to face. Marching mainly at night, and often following mule-tracks across mountain ridges, with his cavalry skilfully deployed to conceal his true direction, he probably felt that he was more than a match for his adversaries.

But one of his aims had been to recruit an army to continue the fight against the enemy. Instead, almost from the first day, his men had begun to desert, sensing the hopelessness of the struggle. Even with the contingent that Forbes had brought with him, his force was now reduced to about 2500 and his march was beginning to look like a retreat.

There was too the daily problem of getting rations for his troops. Usually the towns he passed through had to be compelled to supply him with food and money, in spite of the authority the Roman republic had conferred on him. For them Garibaldi was an unwelcome guest, even though the heaviest burden fell on the monasteries. Only occasionally did he have the good luck to capture supplies destined for the French.

From Todi, Garibaldi marched westwards to Orvieto and, going north from there, crossed the border into Tuscany on July 17. He now had to face the Austrians under his old enemy, General d'Aspre, who was only too anxious to have an opportunity to destroy him. He hoped to find support among the people in Tuscany and this was indeed the case in Cetona, the first town he stopped at, and in Montepulciano.

But although the people were friendly, greeting his arrival with wine and music, there were few new recruits. Reluctantly, as his numbers continued to diminish, Garibaldi was obliged to conclude that he would have to give up his plans for fighting back from the mountains and head for Venice, where Manin still held out against the Austrians.

He marched first to Arezzo, where he found the town gates firmly barred against him. The morale of his troops suffered, but he was unwilling to use force against fellow-Italians. Then, a few days later, on July 28, he had his first encounter with the enemy: the Austrians attacked his rearguard and, in the skirmish that followed, Garibaldi lost some of his cavalry. Even his officers now began to desert.

The following day he arrived at Macerata Feltria. He had decided to seek refuge in the tiny republic of San Marino, which they reached on July 30. The Regent of San Marino was at first reluctant to let them in but his hand was forced when the Austrians, now in hot pursuit, once again attacked Garibaldi's rearguard. Garibaldi crossed the frontier into San Marino without waiting further for permission.

Exhausted by the long march through increasingly mountainous country and by the lack of food, his men had not stood up to the Austrian attack and Garibaldi now decided to disband his remaining 1500 volunteers. On July 31 he wrote his last order of the day:

'Soldiers, I release you from your duty to follow me. You are free to go back to your homes. But remember that Italy remains in slavery. The Roman war for the independence of Italy is over.'

Meanwhile Belzoppi, the Regent of San Marino, had negotiated terms of surrender for the Garibaldini, which even included safe conduct for Garibaldi and Anita. But these terms had to be ratified by the Austrian commander-in-chief, and Garibaldi was doubtful about the outcome. Perhaps, in any case, he had already decided to try to escape.

His main concern must have been for Anita. In spite of her pregnancy, she had stood up well to the hardships of the retreat, behaving much as she had done during the campaigns of Rio Grande. In the last few days, however, she had developed some kind of fever and Garibaldi wanted her to stay behind in San Marino. She refused. "You want to leave me!" she said accusingly.

And so, on the night of July 31, when Garibaldi, with the help of a guide, managed to slip through the Austrian lines with 200 of his men, Anita rode at his side as usual.

The following evening the tiny band of Garibaldini reached Cesenatico, a small fishing port on the Adriatic coast. Garibaldi's plan now was to sail up the coast to Venice, about a hundred miles to the north . . . and for this he needed boats.

The local fishermen, just returned from their day's work, were reluctant to risk their lives against the Austrian navy, but Garibaldi was in no mood to accept refusal. He forced them to embark at the point of the sword, even though a gale was blowing up. Meanwhile Colonel Forbes guarded the entrance to the town, which was barricaded against the Austrians, until everyone was safely aboard.

During the next twenty-four hours they made good progress up the coast. They were short of water, however, and Anita was now seriously ill. Then, fifty miles south of Venice, in the area of Lake Comacchio, they ran into an Austrian naval patrol.

It was a bright moonlit night; the Austrians saw them immediately and opened fire. The fishermen made little effort to get clear. Only three of the thirteen boats, with about thirty men in each, managed to reach the beach. Anita was so ill that she had to be carried ashore.

Garibaldi told his men to disperse and make their escape as best they could. One man, Captain Culiolo, nicknamed 'Leggiero', who had served in the Italian legion in Montevideo, was allowed to stay with him and while Leggiero went ahead to explore, Garibaldi remained hidden with Anita in a maize field.

But someone else, apart from the Austrians, was trying to find them. Gino Bonnet, a prominent landowner in the area who sympathised with the republican cause and had fought in the siege of Rome, had seen the Austrians fire on the fishing boats and had guessed that the Garibaldini might be in them.

He had also seen the three boats heading for the shore and realised that they were in danger. For they had landed not on the mainland but on an island, and would have to be taken off by boat.

Bonnet met up with Leggiero and together they went back to the field where Garibaldi and Anita lay hidden. He took them first to a nearby farm, where Anita was put to bed. Bonnet was convinced that she needed urgent medical attention and should remain hidden until she got better. Garibaldi himself must give up the idea of going to Venice and make his escape without her. Reluctantly Garibaldi agreed.

During the night, arrangements were made to take Anita on a cart to another farm. But when Garibaldi told her that she must stay behind, she burst out again, begging him not to abandon her.

"How can I leave her behind?" Garibaldi said to Bonnet. "You cannot imagine how much she has sacrificed for me. I owe her so much gratitude and love."

Bonnet then arranged with two fishermen to take Garibaldi, Anita and Leggiero off the island in their boat. Garibaldi had by this time changed into an old suit and perhaps had also shaved off his beard. But as soon as the fishermen recognised their passengers, they abandoned them on a small island in the middle of the lake, where, cold and shivering, they spent the night in a hut.

Once again Garibaldi was lucky. The fishermen told everyone — except the Austrians — what they had done. Bonnet found out what had happened and managed to arrange for another fisherman called Guidi to take them from the island to the other side of the lake.

It was now eight o'clock in the morning and Anita was barely conscious. Guidi went off to get help and returned with a cart with a mattress in it. On this Anita was carried several miles to another farm in Mandriole, which was managed by two brothers called Ravaglia, both republicans. Almost at the same moment the doctor arrived.

Anita was carried into the house on the mattress. She had not spoken for some time and, as she was being taken up the stairs, she was seized with a convulsion. 'Even as we laid her on the bed,' Garibaldi wrote in his memoirs, 'I seemed to see the look of death on her face. I felt her pulse. It was no longer beating. There in front of me was the mother of my children . . . a corpse!'

The doctor confirmed that she was dead. Anita had made her last journey at her husband's side.

Garibaldi in 1860

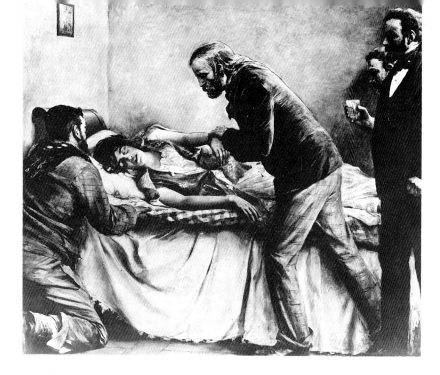

The death of Anita in 1849

Garibaldi in England: arriving in Southampton, 3 April 1864

Garibaldi's entry into Naples, 22 September 1860

Garibaldi's house on Caprera, 1861

The defence of Rome

Labels on map:
North
Aurelian Wall
Lateran Gate
Tiber
River
Villa Spada
Villa Savorelli
Aurelian Wall
Porta San Pancrazio
Janiculum Hill
Villa Corsini
Vatican
St Peter's
Villa Pamfili

0   mile

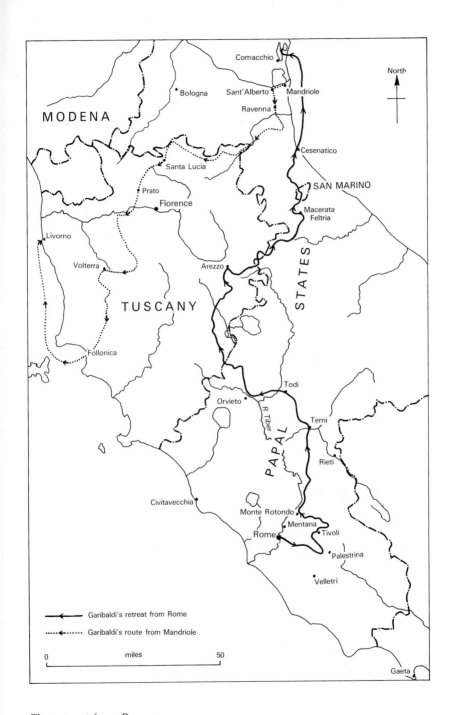

North

Comacchio

Bologna

Sant'Alberto · ·Mandriole
Ravenna

MODENA

Cesenatico

Santa Lucia

SAN MARINO

Prato
Florence

Macerata
Feltria

Livorno

Volterra

Arezzo

TUSCANY

S
T
A
T
E
S

Follonica

Todi

Orvieto ·
R. Tiber

Terni

P
A
P
A
L

Rieti

Civitavecchia

Monte Rotondo

Mentana
Rome · · Tivoli

Palestrina

Velletri

Garibaldi's retreat from Rome

Garibaldi's route from Mandriole

0   miles   50

Gaeta

The retreat from Rome

Anita Garibaldi

Giuseppe Mazzini, 1844

Victor Emanuel

Cavour, 1860

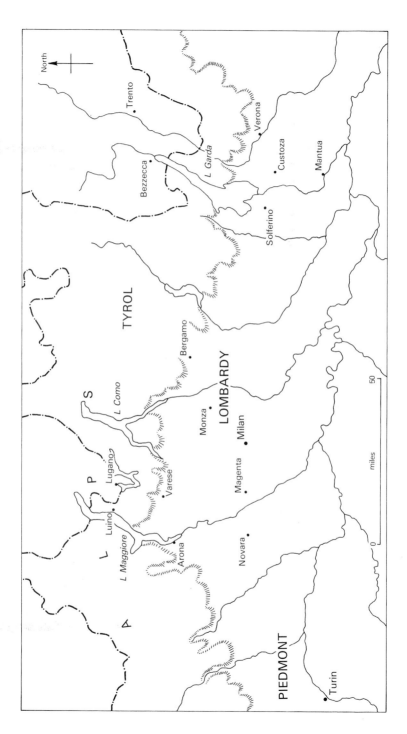

Northern Italian states and the Alps

15
The Wanderer

So here he was, a middle-aged exile in Tangier, writing his memoirs and filling out his days with hunting and small talk, grateful for the company of the consul and his dog.

Strange to think that only a few months before he'd been leading the French and the Austrians a merry dance across the mountains.

Not that the finale had been so merry, the evening she'd breathed her last in the farmhouse by the lake's edge.

He'd never forget the look on the children's faces when he came home without her. They'd pressed forward, crowding him, only Menotti (nine now and quite the little man) holding somewhat aloof.

Teresita had tossed her golden curls. "She must have told you in Rome how good I was, didn't she?" He had nodded, choking back tears, waiting for the question he knew must follow. "And where is Mama?"

His own mother, grim-faced in the background, pursed her lips as if to say: "Enough said! Don't lie to the child or you'll regret it."

And the truth was too awful to tell: that he, a soldier and a leader of men, had left their mother unburied and had scuttled off to save his own skin.

As he kissed Teresita, he'd seen the reproachful look on her face. And he saw it again each time he looked at her that day until he left. And he saw it still in his mind's eye.

Did it matter that the life of the republic had been so brief? No! It lived on and would one day be born again.

But nothing could bring her back. She was dead — and so, in the end, he had had his revenge.

On September 4 1849, a month after Anita's death, Garibaldi and Leggiero reached Spezia, in the Kingdom of Sardinia. They had travelled for two days up the coast in a fishing vessel and from there they went on to Chiavari — where Garibaldi's father had been born. It was from Chiavari that, shortly afterwards, the news was given to the world that the hero of the ill-fated Roman Republic had managed to elude the Austrians.

Even before Anita could be buried, Garibaldi and Leggiero had been hurried away to the nearby village of Sant'Alberto, and then taken south and hidden among the pine forests outside Ravenna.

The general plan of their helpers was to take them in the direction least expected — towards Tuscany. For the next two weeks they were passed under cover of darkness from one band of republican sympathisers to the next, all risking their lives because the Austrians had proclaimed that anyone caught helping the Garibaldini would be shot.

At one point they lost contact with their helpers between Bologna and Florence and had to try to carry on on their own. They hired a cart and, as they travelled along the main road towards Florence, there were Austrians all around them. Later that day, in Santa Lucia, they even shared an inn with their pursuers.

They had gone into the inn for coffee. When the Austrian troops entered 'I just put my head down on the table and pretended to be asleep!' Garibaldi records in his memoirs. In another version of the incident, the landlord's daughter recognised Garibaldi when he came in, warned him of the Austrians and so helped to save his life.

Meanwhile although Garibaldi did not know it, Anita's hastily buried body had been discovered. It had been dug up and partly eaten by some dogs. The farmworkers who had helped him to escape were charged with murder and were released only when the doctor who had come to see Anita admitted that he had been present at her death.

For a time, however, the story persisted that Anita had been murdered and the implication was that Garibaldi had killed his pregnant wife because she was hindering his escape.

Bonnet too was arrested. He was held for a time, certain that he was going to be executed, and then quite suddenly released. Colonel Forbes and his men were also lucky: they were treated as prisoners of war and, after being interned in Dalmatia for several months, were allowed to go free.

Others who had taken part in the retreat were less fortunate. Ugo Bassi, a priest who supported the republican cause, though he had never carried arms, was caught in Comacchio. He was taken to Bologna, brutally treated and then shot. Ciceruacchio, too, the revolutionary wineseller from Trastevere, was captured not far from Venice and executed, along with two of his sons, one of them a mere boy of thirteen.

From the inn at Santa Lucia, Garibaldi and Leggiero continued their journey towards Florence, intending to cross the frontier into the Kingdom of Sardinia as soon as possible. Once more luck was on their side. Near Prato, Garibaldi met a young man called Enrico Sequi and decided to put his life in his hands by revealing his identity.

His instinct proved right. Sequi arranged for them to be looked after by another chain of helpers and from Prato they were taken south, towards Volterra and the sea, thus avoiding the Austrians, who were closely guarding the frontier against any fugitives.

Their torturous journey was drawing to a close. Towards the end of August 1849 they reached San Dalmazio, about thirty kilometres from the coast. Here they were hospitably looked after — Garibaldi was always careful to record the names of his benefactors in his memoirs, even mentioning a priest who had helped them earlier in their escape — until arrangements could be made to take them to safety.

Then, on September 1, they set off at night with a group of young men, disguised as hunters and carrying guns. They were heading, through the thick woods, for Follonica, in the Gulf of Sterlino. A little further south, at dawn the following day, with cries of "*Viva l'Italia!*", they went on board a fishing vessel at Cala Martina and were taken to safety.

They were safe from the Austrians but Garibaldi had his doubts — and not without reason — about how they would be received by the authorities in Piedmont. At Livorno he even considered asking for asylum on board a British ship. But, although he knew that he would have to leave Italy, he was determined to see his family first.

At Chiavari he was arrested and taken to Genoa, where he was detained, not uncomfortably, in the ducal palace while a decision was taken about his future. His arrest provoked a storm of protest from politicians on the left, and in a vote of censure the government was overwhelmingly defeated. Garibaldi himself, however, behaved discreetly during this period. His main concern was still to get the opportunity to see his family.

In the end he was allowed to go to Nice for a day to say goodbye to his family and was also offered a small pension, which he accepted on behalf of his mother and his children. Then, on September 16 1849, he left Genoa on the gunboat *Tripoli*, bound for Tunis.

Then began a period of searching for a place of exile. The Bey of Tunis, reluctant to offend the French, declined to let him stay there. Garibaldi returned with the *Tripoli* to Sardinia, where he spent nearly a month on the small island of La Maddalena. It was from La Maddalena that he first saw his future home, the nearby island of Caprera.

Finally, after being turned away from Gibraltar — where the British governor treated him so harshly that, for all his love of the English, Garibaldi was disgusted that 'a representative of England should have kicked a man when he was down' — he was offered refuge in Tangier, where he spent the next seven months.

In Tangier Garibaldi was the house guest of the Sardinian consul, and also became close friends with the English vice-consul, Murray. He spent a good deal of his time on his favourite pastimes of hunting and fishing, and wrote the first version of his autobiography, up to the time he had returned to Italy from Montevideo. More recent events were perhaps still too painful or even too dangerous to write about.

He says in his memoirs that this was a 'happy and tranquil period' of his life — to the extent, he adds, that it is possible for an Italian to be happy in exile. But he must have spent much time brooding over the events of the last few months, especially the death of Anita, and wondering if he would ever be allowed to return.

Eventually, as he well knew, he would have to find a more permanent place of exile, and only the United States seemed to offer any real promise. There at least he would find friends among fellow-Italians in exile and the possibility of work, perhaps even as a sea captain if he took American citizenship.

In June 1850 he left Tangier for Liverpool. His short stay there passed almost unnoticed and a few days later, on June 17, he left for the United States, where he arrived just over a month later.

There was no shortage of hospitality awaiting Garibaldi in New York, but he had no intention of accepting the role of a famous man in exile. He even avoided the reception ceremony arranged in his honour.

For a while he found manual work in a candle factory, set up to help Italian refugees by the rich businessman with whom he lodged, Antonio Meucci. Life was not unpleasant: he had plenty of like-minded friends with whom he could relax, hunting or playing bowls, and there was work to be done, helping other Italian refugees.

But his heart was set on returning to sea and with this in mind he applied for American citizenship. One day, while walking near the port, he even offered to join a ship as an ordinary sailor — but was turned down. This hurt — particularly when he remembered that, only two years before, he had commanded the fleet at Montevideo!

Luckily at this point, in April 1851, a group of friends collected enough money for a ship to be bought in San Francisco, which Garibaldi would take over as captain. The transaction took time, and he was able to travel for a few months through Central America, *en route* to pick up his ship, the *Carmen*, which had been taken down to Lima, in Peru.

In January 1852 he left on a voyage to Canton, with a cargo of guano (the fertiliser which was making Peru rich). One night, as he lay in his cabin during a storm, he dreamt of his mother . . . and of a funeral. A year later he learnt that she had died on that very day, March 19.

He spent over six months in the China seas, where he had some difficulty in getting rid of his cargo. He also had to contend with pirates, much as he did in his youth in the Aegean. He made the return journey via Australia and New Zealand, to avoid storms, and came close to running out of food because the journey took longer than was expected. He finally reached Lima again in January 1853 and from there he returned to Boston and New York.

There was good news for Garibaldi in New York. A coalition government had been formed in Turin under a rising new politician, Count Camillo Cavour. Garibaldi was given to understand that he would be allowed to return home if he gave no trouble. At the same time he obtained command of a new ship, the *Commonwealth*, bound for Genoa via London and Newcastle.

After nearly four years, his exile was unexpectedly drawing to a close.

16
The Farmer

One thing he was sure of: he'd had enough of exile!

Alone in Tangier, he'd had time to think. There, and in New York, it would have been easy to assume the role of 'distinguished exile'. But he'd turned that down and had worked for his living, sending home his savings like any other Italian immigrant.

In the end, though, not even the command of a ship again and those long nights on deck studying the stars could hide from him the emptiness of an exile's life or dispel thoughts of his children growing up without him.

And he was tired of exiles too! They had no attachment to place or person, most of them. At some time in their youth they'd nailed their flag to the mast of a ship and now, prisoners of their own convictions, the ship carried them on.

But there was no end to the voyage and perhaps they did not even want it.

Well, Mazzini wouldn't get round him this time, he'd made his mind up on that score! He'd had enough of madcap schemes which cost young blood and achieved nothing.

No, he was as good a republican as the next man, but from now on he was ready to back Piedmont and the king . . . yes, and even that schemer Cavour . . . if this would help free Italy from the Austrians.

For the moment, though, this exile was simply going home . . . to see his children . . . and find a home for them perhaps.

And — who knows? — he hardly dared think of it, but the thought would not leave him, he might even find a mother for his children . . .

Garibaldi arrived in England on February 11 1854. The press, busy with the war in the Crimea which England and France were waging against the Czar of Russia, scarcely noticed the arrival of the sea captain who, as a revolutionary, had once been hunted half the length of Italy. In any case, London at the time was the home of many distinguished revolutionaries in exile, and during the month he spent there Garibaldi met a number of them, including Mazzini.

Mazzini was hoping to involve Garibaldi in one of his schemes for revolution, which he still believed to be the best way of liberating Italy. One of these plots had failed miserably in Milan only twelve months before, although this did not deter him from dreaming up others. 'Mazzini's watch stopped in 1848,' one writer commented acidly.

But Garibaldi, who had already disagreed with Mazzini over the defence of Rome, now detached himself even further from his former master. Their relations remained cordial, but Garibaldi made it clear that he favoured the approach followed by many moderate republicans, including Manin himself, of working with Cavour and Victor Emmanuel for the liberation of Italy.

"I have been a republican all my life," he told Alexander Herzen, a Russian revolutionary in exile in London, "but it is not a question of a republic at this moment. I know the Italian masses better than Mazzini. I have lived among them all my life. Mazzini knows only the Italian intellectuals."

Mazzini, on his side, was equally cutting about Garibaldi's new allegiance: "He will never start anything for himself," he declared. "He will follow the republicans if we act first, or the monarchists if they do!"

In London, Garibaldi became engaged to a rich widow called Emma Roberts. It was the first hint of romance in his life since Anita's death five years before, though he omits all mention of it in his autobiography.

Emma was completely different from Anita: she was sophisticated and intelligent, and enjoyed moving in society. In spite of her sympathy for the Italian cause and her admiration for Garibaldi — which she shared with many Englishwomen of her time — she was an improbable companion for a man who prided himself on being a simple sailor, and the engagement never led to marriage.

From London, Garibaldi sailed to Newcastle, to collect a cargo of coal, and during his three-week stay there, he met the radical family, the Cowens. The Cowens were friends of Mazzini and great supporters of the Italian struggle for freedom.

When he left, Garibaldi was presented with a sword and was moved to learn that it had been bought from pennies contributed by working men. "I am a worker like yourselves," he said in his speech of thanks. "One day Italy will be a nation and if England ever needs my help, I will gladly use this sword in her defence!"

On his return voyage, he spent a few more days with his friends in London and then sailed for Genoa, where he arrived on May 7 1854.

Garibaldi's future, as he was well aware, depended to a large extent on how well he could get on with Cavour, who had already become suspicious when he heard that Garibaldi was mixing with revolutionaries like Mazzini in London.

Cavour came from an aristocratic Piedmontese family and as a young man had travelled widely, studying industrial developments and parliamentary systems, particularly in England and France. After making a good deal of money by introducing advanced farming methods on his estates, he entered politics as a moderate liberal and became prime minister at the age of forty-two.

Cavour wanted to see Austria expelled from Italian soil. But his concept of Italian unity at the time meant little more than expanding the Kingdom of Sardinia to include Lombardy and possibly Venice. For these schemes perhaps there was a use for someone like Garibaldi, if he could be kept apart from Mazzini and did not encourage the king to become a dictator. For Cavour was a firm believer in parliamentary government — provided parliament, when required, could be used to serve his own purposes.

Garibaldi, sensitive to the changed political climate and perhaps genuinely wishing to lead a quiet life, at least for a while, kept clear of Mazzini's rash ventures. He spent his first summer back home with his family. The children were growing up rapidly, with Menotti, now fourteen, away at a military college. He left Teresita staying with relatives but took charge of Ricciotti, the youngest, even giving him his first lessons in writing. He lived much as he had done at Tangier, following his favourite pastimes of walking and hunting in the hills and fishing.

The following year, in the spring of 1855, Emma Roberts came on a visit, bringing with her a young woman, Jessie White, as companion. Jessie, who had studied in Paris and was already a dedicated radical ('a subversive by vocation' in the words of one unfriendly critic), soon became one of Garibaldi's most enthusiastic admirers and ultimately one of his biographers. Garibaldi did not change his simple way of life for his sophisticated fiancée, although they later went on holiday together to Sardinia.

Garibaldi's thoughts were turning increasingly towards finding a permanent home for himself and his family, and at one stage he had the idea of settling in Sardinia. Eventually he chose the tiny island of Caprera, close to La Maddalena, where he had stayed briefly on his way into exile. Caprera was convenient in more than one respect: it was isolated . . . but not too far from the mainland.

In the autumn he went to sea again, trading mainly along the coast. But, although he had got back his master's certificate, he was no longer interested in a life at sea, perhaps because he was now nearly fifty and suffered from frequent attacks of arthritis.

His main concern was to raise money to buy land on Caprera, which he was able to do when his younger brother Felice died and left him some money. Combined with his own savings, he had enough to buy about half of the island.

The following year, with the help of Menotti and some friends, Garibaldi began building a house — a one-storey building with four rooms of the kind he had seen and liked in South America — and preparing the rocky soil of the island for farming.

In due course he managed to produce a variety of crops — cereals, vegetables and fruit — and also to rear animals, though it turned out to be an expensive and uphill struggle. But, in spite of all the problems, he enjoyed his life as a farmer and eventually bought the other half of the island, with the help of his English admirers.

This quiet life on Caprera continued until 1859, but, however important it was to him at the time, it is dismissed in his memoirs as being of 'no interest'. At one point he seemed likely to be drawn into a daring plot to snatch some political prisoners from the island of Santo Stefano, where they had been imprisoned by the King of Naples. But the scheme was abandoned when the boat, paid for and built in England, was wrecked.

In 1857 Garibaldi gave up the sea completely and from then on devoted himself entirely to farming. He played no part in the revolts which Mazzini organised that year, both in Genoa and in the south of Italy — and which failed as miserably as earlier ones had done. His friend Jessie White was involved, however, and afterwards married the Italian revolutionary Alberto Mario.

Garibaldi's relationship with Emma had come to an end in 1856, though they remained good friends, however, and continued to correspond. Other women now came into his life. The first was Battistina Ravello, a peasant girl from Nice who had gone to Caprera to run his house and look after Teresita. In time this plain uneducated girl became his mistress and in 1859 they had a daughter, whom he called Anita.

A more romantic figure was the Baroness Maria Esperance von Schwartz, who first visited him on Caprera in 1857. The baroness, twice married and something of an adventuress, wrote under the name of Elpis Melena (or *Black Hope*) and was eager to get permission to translate Garibaldi's memoirs, brought up to date, into German.

Garibaldi was not keen on the idea, but he was attracted by the young baroness, and also flattered perhaps by her unconcealed admiration. They went on to exchange love letters and, when she visited Caprera again the following year, Garibaldi asked 'his Speranza', as he now called her, to become 'a second mother to his children'.

Speranza asked for time to think it over. She liked and admired Garibaldi, but she had also noticed that the relationship between him and his housekeeper was 'not quite straightforward'. The romantic attachment between them continued into the following year, when they met more than once on the mainland.

Then, in 1860, Garibaldi suddenly married the young Marchesina Raimondi, with whom he had become hopelessly infatuated. But he discovered on their wedding day that she had been unfaithful to him with one of his own officers and they parted company the same day. After this disastrous marriage Speranza became, like Emma, another of his 'good friends'.

By this time, however, political events had already conspired to drag Garibaldi away from his quiet retreat on Caprera.

17
The Patriot

He'd known all along, of course, it couldn't go on for ever, this quiet life on Caprera.

The Austrians were still on Italian soil and, though he kept himself fit — fighting, it amused him to tell his visitors, rocks and stones and skirmishing with his neighbour's goats — time was passing and, frankly, he wasn't getting any younger!

More than once he'd felt the urge to join one of Mazzini's insurrections. All he asked for, like any military commander, was a reasonable chance of success. But that was something Mazzini never gave a thought to. The waste, the futility of it, made him go hot with anger.

Now the call had come and it must be urgent, for why else should they send a boat to take him to the mainland?

But what was he up to, that cunning old fox Cavour? Perhaps there was some truth after all in what Mazzini had claimed — that a plot had been hatched with the French against the Austrians. Cavour had denied it, of course, but then . . . all politicians lied through their teeth.

Well, whatever it was, they'd find him ready and waiting. He'd get them their volunteers, if that was what they wanted. He only had to raise the flag and they'd pour in in their thousands, eager to serve under 'the general'!

And could they then deny him his rightful share of the glory?

Cavour, meanwhile, had been making steady progress with his plans to secure Lombardy and Venice.

He recognised that, for a war against Austria, France's help was essential and he was prepared to go to almost any length to influence Louis Napoleon. He even arranged for his cousin, the beautiful Countess Castiglione, to become the emperor's mistress.

There was a temporary setback when an Italian revolutionary, Felice Orsini, tried to assassinate Louis Napoleon and his wife outside the Paris Opera House. Orsini was tried and executed . . .

but Louis Napoleon became an even stronger supporter of the Italian cause.

In July 1858 Cavour and Louis Napoleon met secretly at Plombières, in eastern France, to make their final plans. Austria was to be provoked into attacking Sardinia; France would come to her rescue and Austria would be defeated. Sardinia would be given Lombardy and Venice, and France would get Savoy and Nice. Cavour was unhappy about giving away Nice, which was Garibaldi's birthplace, but Louis Napoleon insisted that it was part of the bargain.

Cavour first met Garibaldi in August 1856. The meeting was cordial, although Garibaldi appears to have had no illusions about Cavour. 'He's like one of those ancient noblemen who look down on the common people!' he wrote.

But he was convinced that he and Cavour must work together for the sake of Italy. A year later, he became honorary vice-president of the Italian National Party, which promoted the very ideas Cavour stood for — especially war against Austria.

In December 1858 Cavour summoned Garibaldi to Turin and revealed his plans for provoking Austria into a war. Garibaldi was invited to raise volunteers . . . and no mention, naturally, was made of Nice.

Garibaldi was delighted and rushed off to tell his radical friends. "At last they've agreed to act!" he told Dr Bertani in Genoa, his face radiant with joy. "I've been given permission at the highest level to tell all my friends to be ready."

His friends, including Bertani, thought that Garibaldi was being duped. Mazzini had already exposed Cavour's secret deal with Louis Napoleon, though Cavour of course had denied it. In the end, however, many of them, including Bertani, were persuaded to lend their support.

In February 1859 Garibaldi was once again asked to go to Turin to raise a volunteer army, which would be called *I Cacciatori delle Alpi*. He himself was given the rank of major-general. He also met the king — and reminded him and Cavour that 'the help of foreign armies must always be paid for'.

It did not take Garibaldi long to discover that he was being used. His name was drawing in recruits like a magnet while *he* had 'to keep out of sight, to appear and disappear when required', as he wrote in his memoirs. The best recruits were enrolled in the regular army, while he got those 'least fit to carry arms'. He got little equipment: only old-fashioned weapons and no artillery.

When he complained, he was told the matter would be looked into. In fact, neither Cavour nor the military had any intention of doing anything about it. Garibaldi was too dangerous a man to be allowed to command a large and well-equipped army.

At least he had some excellent officers — men like Medici and Bixio, who had fought at Rome. He also had two very efficient companies of scouts and sharpshooters. Best of all, he was able to inspire his volunteers — a mixed lot, as always — with enthusiasm and courage. Garibaldi knew how to get the best out of virtually untrained men.

Cavour's carefully laid plans nearly came undone when the British persuaded the French to ask the Italians to disarm and to refer the Italian question to a peace conference. Cavour was in despair — until the Austrians delivered an ultimatum, giving Sardinia three days to demobilise. Sardinia refused and on April 27 the Austrians declared war.

It was the perfect conclusion for the scenario that Cavour had worked out with Louis Napoleon the previous summer at Plombières.

The Austrians advanced so quickly and in such large numbers that it looked as if they would overrun Piedmont before the French arrived. Luckily, held up by bad weather and indecision, they delayed their attack. Garibaldi, whose volunteer force was intended to be used for guerrilla activities, won two small victories against the Austrians. His prestige increased considerably during this campaign — thus making him more dangerous in the eyes of Cavour and the military.

Then the news came through that the Austrians had been defeated at Magenta on June 4 and that Victor Emmanuel and Louis Napoleon had entered Milan. The Austrians were allowed to withdraw and fell back towards Lake Garda. Then, on June 24, French and Austrian troops came into conflict, almost accidentally, near Solferino. A major battle followed, with huge losses on both sides.

It was a victory for the allies, but at such a cost that Louis Napoleon decided to put an end to the war. On July 10 1859 he concluded a treaty with the Austrians, virtually excluding the Italians from the negotiations. Austria agreed to give up Lombardy, though to avoid humiliation it came to Sardinia via France. Austria was, however, allowed to keep Venice, in spite of the agreement at Plombières.

Cavour was furious when he heard, and resigned as prime minister. "I won't allow the treaty to be executed," he stormed. "Never! Never!" He lost his temper in the presence of the king and even threatened to become a revolutionary himself. Then Cavour began to shout at the king himself and was ordered to leave the room.

In spite of popular indignation against the treaty, Garibaldi himself made no protest. Probably he was disappointed at the role he had been allowed to play in the war, which at one point had put his volunteers in great danger. In any case, his aims did not coincide with those of Cavour, who was chiefly interested in expanding the Kingdom of Sardinia. Garibaldi wanted nothing less than a united Italy.

The opportunity to carry on working for this soon presented itself. When the war with Austria broke out, the central Italian states of Modena, Parma and Tuscany had driven out their foreign rulers and set up revolutionary governments. Together with Romagna, one of the Papal States which had also revolted, they now asked to become part of the Kingdom of Sardinia.

Garibaldi was invited to become commander-in-chief of their combined forces and when the *Cacciatori delle Alpi* were disbanded, many officers and men followed him to his new appointment. Conditions for liberating other papal states must have seemed favourable.

But Garibaldi's hands were tied from the start: instead of being commander-in-chief, he found that he had been placed under a cautious Sardinian general. All the same, this did not prevent him from calling upon all Italians to arm themselves. A million rifles and a million men were what he demanded!

He was under pressure from the radicals — perhaps even secretly supported by Victor Emmanuel — to invade the Marches. News came that revolution had broken out. But when he decided to stage an invasion in support, he found that his men had been instructed to disobey him. The news of revolution was false, it later turned out.

Shortly afterwards, he was summoned to Turin by the king. His conduct, he was told, was causing international alarm and he was asked to resign. He declined an appointment in the Sardinian army and, after denouncing what he called 'the miserable foxlike policy that was holding back the progress of the Italian movement', he decided to return to Caprera.

Events were now bringing him closer to open opposition to Cavour, who had become prime minister again. In March 1860 the secret agreement at Plombières, which involved giving Savoy and Nice to France, was finally revealed. Although it was subject to a plebiscite, many Sardinians were angry — not least Garibaldi, who would now become 'a stranger in his own country'. To make matters worse, only a few months before he had brought the body of Anita to Nice from Mandriole.

Garibaldi had no difficulty in getting himself elected as a deputy for Nice and denounced the secret agreement as unconstitutional. His speech was applauded, but the plebiscite went ahead, with an overwhelming majority in favour of annexation to France.

It left Garibaldi angry both with Cavour and parliament — and even more determined and ready to act on his own if the opportunity presented itself.

73

18
The Liberator

And so the time for action had come at last!

After weeks of waiting and endless argument — which at one point had nearly cost him his good name — they were finally on their way to liberate Sicily, on two steamships 'borrowed' for the occasion!

It was quite like old times! Somehow he felt better on board ship. The sea was his element and gave him confidence.

And he was going to need it! A thousand men against the Bourbon army . . . who knew the island backwards. And at this point he didn't even know where he was going to land!

Well, he could think about that later. His men needed training, and that wasn't something he relished. Bixio had already started in on his lot, from what he'd heard, even breaking a plate over the head of a man who'd questioned his word. Now that was discipline for you!

Well, he'd take a gentler line himself. Put on his general's uniform to impress them and give them all a pep talk. That and a spot of rifle drill might do the trick.

At least they'd got a few rifles now and some ammunition . . . And they had their bayonets to put the fear of God into the Bourbons. Twenty thousand of them, though . . .

It would be all right on the day, that he felt sure of! Down there in the island of almonds, they were going to make Italy . . . or die.

Ever since Garibaldi's return from exile in 1854, Mazzini had been trying to involve him in plots to liberate the south from its Bourbon ruler, the King of Naples.

The main target was Sicily. There was unrest in the island, brought about by oppression and poverty. Few Sicilians served in the Neapolitan army. 'Better a pig than a soldier!' ran the Sicilian saying. There was also the hatred of the peasants for the landowners to be exploited. Many Sicilian exiles actively plotted with Mazzini, though their aim was independence for their island rather than unity with the mainland.

But Garibaldi obstinately refused to support any venture that did not seem reasonably sure of success. He also demanded evidence of strong internal support. Revolts had failed in the past and his concern, he argued, was to avoid unnecessary loss of life.

The situation changed in May 1859 with the death of King Ferdinand of Naples — nicknamed 'Bomba' because he had once bombed his subjects into submission. It seemed the appropriate moment to end oppression and bring in a liberal constitution. But his weak-minded son, King Francis, hesitated: he made a few concessions but, like his father, he continued to rely on the police to keep his subjects in order. The Sicilians became more determined than ever to stage a revolution against Naples.

They had already appealed to Garibaldi to help them in their struggle, but his reply had been cautious: 'Unite yourselves to our programme — Italy and Victor Emmanuel,' he had written back. 'If you can do it with any chance of success, then rise! If not, work at unity and strengthen yourselves.'

It was not quite the response the Sicilians were expecting — and the pressure to involve Garibaldi directly went on. It was recognised that his support was essential, and the Mazzinians too were determined to make him change his mind.

Mazzini had already sent a leading Sicilian exile, Francesco Crispi, to stir up unrest in the island. Then, in March 1860 he wrote to the Sicilians: 'Wait? For what? Dare — and you will be followed! But dare in the name of national unity. Garibaldi is bound to come to your help.' At the same time another Sicilian, Rosolino Pilo, was sent to start a revolt — and to announce that Garibaldi was on his way!

But by this time the Sicilians had already decided to go ahead on their own. On April 4 a revolt broke out in Palermo, and later in the cities of Messina and Catania. It was put down without much effort by the Bourbon troops, but it continued to smoulder on in the countryside, where Pilo worked to keep it alive.

In the middle of April Garibaldi agreed to lead an invasion of Sicily and for three weeks he stayed in Genoa at the villa of an old friend, Agosto Vecchi, making arrangements for the expedition while volunteers poured in from all parts of Italy.

After years of restraint, he had finally committed himself to action!

Cavour, once again prime minister, did not openly either oppose or support the expedition. Probably he would have liked to prevent Garibaldi from leading it; he may even have wished to get rid of him — but he did not dare have him arrested.

The number of volunteers continued to grow and Garibaldi decided to sail on April 28. Cavour had authorised the release of 1500 rifles from the stores of the National Society, but these turned out to be old and rusty and were mostly useless. Garibaldi had been refused weapons bought from the 'Million Rifles' fund — money which he himself had collected — but decided to make the best of a bad job. At least the antiquated rifles could be used for bayonet charges!

Then, on April 27, a telegram in code arrived, which Crispi decoded. 'Complete failure in the provinces and in the city of Palermo . . . Do not start!' The revolt in Sicily had failed!

The depressing news was debated at the villa. Should the expedition be called off? The hot-heads, Crispi and Bixio, were in favour of going ahead. Garibaldi wanted to wait for further news. Hearing that he had backed down, many of the volunteers were angry. Some even began to leave for home.

Crispi had another go at decoding the telegram. He had made a mistake, he announced. In fact the revolt in the provinces was still being maintained — as other telegrams showed! Crispi almost certainly invented this new version to get Garibaldi to change his mind, and the stratagem worked. "Let's start, then!" Garibaldi told them.

The departure date was fixed for May 5. Arrangements were made to take over two steamships, the *Piemonte* and the *Lombardo*, with the connivance of one of the directors of the shipping company. At the last moment Cavour, worried about international opinion, tried to persuade Victor Emmanuel to stop the expedition; but the king supported Garibaldi — against his own minister.

On May 6 the two ships set off down the coast. Their decks were crowded with men who had little to eat and who were feeling the effects of the rough sea. Garibaldi, who was in charge of the *Piemonte*, put on his general's uniform to review his men and was pleasantly surprised to find that they numbered over a thousand.

Apart from Sicilians, the volunteers came mostly from cities in the north — Genoa, Milan and Bergamo. Most wore civilian clothes; hardly any the famous red shirts. As in the past, the volunteers were a mixed bunch, and included many students, doctors and lawyers. There were teachers and writers as well as working men — bakers, builders and barbers! Several of the volunteers were over sixty, while the youngest was only twelve. There was also one woman — Crispi's mistress.

The expedition was short of money and weapons and, in the confusion of the departure, the ammunition had been left behind!

Garibaldi, deeply involved in training his volunteers and writing a battle hymn, was not greatly worried. The ships put in at Ortobello, in the Gulf of Talamone, where the commander of the garrison was induced to part with some ammunition and three small cannons. Coal, food and water were also provided and on May 9 the expedition finally left for Sicily.

Garibaldi had, at this stage, no precise idea where he was going to land. He knew the Neapolitans had a large army on the island, but he felt supremely confident.

The place finally selected was Marsala and it proved to be an excellent choice. On May 10, the day before Garibaldi arrived, the garrison had been temporarily withdrawn, and two warships guarding the harbour suddenly left port. There were also two British warships in the harbour, sent to protect the lives of English residents. Afterwards it was suggested that the British had actually helped Garibaldi. The expedition 'was wrapped in British banknotes', it was claimed.

Garibaldi sailed directly into the harbour with his own ship and began landing his men. Bixio's ship ran aground near the mouth of the harbour and his men had to be brought ashore in small boats. At this point the Neapolitan warships returned, but they were too late to prevent a successful landing.

Once ashore, the Garibaldini cut the lines at the telegraph office — though not before a message had been sent off to confuse the enemy.

Shortly afterwards, Garibaldi was proclaimed 'Dictator of Sicily', with authority to rule the island in the name of Victor Emmanuel.

The following day, Garibaldi left for Salemi, where he learnt that an army of 3000 Neapolitans was waiting for him at Calatafimi, under the command of the aged General Landi. One of Landi's commanders was in a strong position on a hilltop, with 2000 well-armed troops. But, whatever the odds, Garibaldi knew that he must show that he could defeat the Bourbons.

The side of the hill on which the Neapolitan troops were positioned was lined with terraces. His volunteers were able to shelter and take breath behind these walls as they fought their way laboriously up the hillside, but by the time they reached the last terrace, they were exhausted and desperately in need of water.

It was a crucial moment. The enemy was so close that they were able to throw stones down on them. Bixio wanted to retreat. Garibaldi would not hear of it: he knew that they must win. "Today we make Italy — or die!" he declared. Struck by one of the stones, he shouted that the Neapolitans had run out of ammunition — and ordered the final charge.

The fighting was fierce — fiercer than he had ever before experienced in Italy — but in the end the Neapolitans gave way and retreated towards Calatafimi. The Garibaldini had 30 dead and 150 wounded — a little more than the enemy — but a decisive victory had been won.

Garibaldi was now in a position to advance on Palermo, only thirty miles away. Wherever he went, he was greeted like a hero — almost as a god — and joined by an increasing number of volunteers.

Even so, the capture of the capital, well defended by Bourbon troops, must have seemed an almost impossible task. He could not hope to defeat an army of over 20,000 in open battle. Somehow or other, he decided, he must try to get inside the city, where the inhabitants could help to pin down the enemy with barricades and home-made weapons.

Garibaldi marched his volunteers to a position in the hills southeast of Palermo. There he waited several days, in close contact throughout with conspirators in the city. Camp-fires were also lit in the hills to confuse the enemy. The Neapolitan commander, General Lanza, believed that Garibaldi had retreated into the interior and sent a large detachment of 3500 soldiers in pursuit. Everyone in Palermo seemed to know where Garibaldi was — except the Neapolitans!

Soon after midnight on May 27, Garibaldi's troops began to enter Palermo. They met with hardly any opposition. The Sicilians rose to support them and by midday the revolutionaries controlled the city, with Lanza and his men shut up in the royal palace and the cathedral.

The fighting, however, was not yet over. For three more days the Bourbon troops continued to bombard the city and make murderous attacks on the civilian population. Garibaldi's chief worry was his shortage of ammunition. What he did not know was that the Bourbons were desperately short of food and medical supplies.

Much to his surprise he received a letter addressed to 'His Excellency, General Garibaldi'! It was from Lanza asking for a cease-fire so that a truce could be discussed.

A meeting was arranged on board an English warship in the harbour. Garibaldi agreed to a short truce of twenty-four hours — during which time he got together as much ammunition as possible. Even at this stage, Sardinian ships in the harbour refused him help.

The truce was twice extended for nearly a week. Barricades in the streets were strengthened and there was news too of risings in other parts of the island.

Then, on June 6, the Neapolitans agreed to capitulate, on condition that they were allowed to sail back to Naples. Most left the following day, and Palermo was in the hands of the revolutionaries.

By a combination of good luck and daring, Garibaldi had won Sicily for the King of Sardinia — and had taken the unity of Italy one stage further.

With the capture of Palermo came a change of heart in Turin. Cavour allowed more volunteers to be recruited, 3000 of whom arrived in June under Medici. He also sent La Farina, a Sicilian who had formerly run the National Society on his behalf, to take over the government of the island.

But Garibaldi had already appointed his cabinet under Crispi. It included conservatives, so that it could not be said that he was favouring the radicals. However, he firmly refused to hand over to Piedmont at this stage, suspecting that Cavour might try to prevent him from liberating other parts of the mainland, and La Farina was sent back to Turin.

For the six weeks that he governed Sicily, Garibaldi tried to be fair to all parties. He introduced land reforms, but forbade the peasants to seize property from landlords. Many were disappointed, but he was still a great hero in Palermo. He made a great impression with his simple life-style and by attending mass in the cathedral.

Meanwhile, as he prepared for the next stage of his campaign, the number of his volunteers increased until he had about 10,000 men under his command. Many of these were foreigners. In England, in particular, he enjoyed great popularity at all levels of society, and there were numerous schemes to collect money on his behalf.

In order to cross to the mainland, Garibaldi had to gain possession of the area around Messina, which was still under the control of Bourbon troops. In the middle of July he sent three columns, two of them under Bixio and Medici, to attack the Neapolitans, and by a clever manoeuvre Medici managed to shut up a considerable body of them on the promontory of Milazzo. Garibaldi arrived from Palermo with further support and on July 30 a long-drawn-out battle was fought between the two forces.

After eight hours' hard fighting the Garibaldini finally fought their way into the city of Milazzo and the Neapolitan garrison surrendered. Garibaldi's losses were heavy: nearly 800 dead.

His victory, however, persuaded the remainder of the Neapolitans to capitulate, with the exception of those in the citadel of Messina, which held out for over a year. Garibaldi was now in control of the Straits of Messina, as well as the rest of the island, and could prepare his assault on the mainland.

19
The Dictator

Against all the odds they'd taken Palermo, then, and the Neapolitans had left, grateful to be able to escape with their skins intact.

Of course there'd been luck in it right the way through. But it had taken skill too . . . and the determination to make Italy.

He'd trusted the Sicilians and he'd been right. They'd flocked in in their thousands to join him, eager to have a crack at the Bourbon bully-boys. They'd helped him win, though it wouldn't do to look too closely at some of the things they'd done.

The English sailors too had been on his side, whatever their motives . . .

Only the Sardinians, his own people, had stood on the sidelines, awaiting the outcome. But as soon as Palermo was in the bag, Cavour had promptly sent his own man to take over, expecting Sicily to be handed over on a plate!

Well, let him wait! He'd govern Sicily himself for a while — dictator in the name of the king — and he'd show them all that Garibaldi was a just and able man.

Meanwhile, it was time to be moving on . . . towards the next goal, Naples . . . and Rome perhaps. But first there was the problem of getting his men across these straits . . .

Garibaldi waited almost a month before he crossed to the mainland. The three-mile-wide Straits of Messina were well guarded by the Neapolitan navy, and the mainland itself was defended by over 15,000 Bourbon troops. One false move and everything could be lost. Garibaldi would often shut himself up alone in the lighthouse on the Faro to brood on this situation.

In a letter from Victor Emmanuel he had been forbidden to cross to the mainland, though these written instructions were probably countermanded by verbal ones, telling him to go ahead. Cavour as usual was playing a double game. After Garibaldi's triumph in Sicily, he wanted to deprive him of the honour of liberating Naples. It would not be right for the king to receive Naples from Garibaldi's hand: the king's crown would shine with reflected light, Cavour maintained.

However, Cavour's main concern at the time was to head off an alternative attack on the Papal States, which Garibaldi, under the influence of Bertani (who had stayed behind in Genoa to recruit more volunteers) may well have been considering. Cavour therefore stopped all further recruitment and ordered the remaining volunteers to be taken to Sicily. Any idea of an attack on the Papal States now had to be abandoned.

Garibaldi had already tried a raid on the mainland in the hope of establishing a foothold, but this had not met with success. Bixio, meanwhile, had been given the task of secretly assembling a force near Taormina, which now numbered 3500 men.

On August 18 Garibaldi visited Messina, perhaps as a way of covering up his real intentions, and then went on to join Bixio in Taormina. From there, the same night, the Garibaldini made a thirty-mile crossing in two ships, the *Torino* and the *Franklin*, and landed at Melito, thus eluding the Neapolitan navy, which was waiting for them in the Straits.

The Neapolitans, who had good troops but poor officers, seemed unable to take any decisive action against him. On August 21 Garibaldi attacked Reggio di Calabria and forced the Neapolitans to take refuge in the castle. He then defeated a stronger force that had come to the rescue before getting the Neapolitans in Reggio to surrender.

More volunteers under Cosenz now crossed to the mainland, bringing Garibaldi's strength up to over five thousand. The peasants too began to revolt and form partisan groups. The main Neapolitan force of over eight thousand retreated in disorder and Garibaldi pursued them with a much smaller mobile troop, way ahead of his own army.

Trapped between Garibaldi and the partisans, who were seeking revenge, the Neapolitans surrendered at Soveria-Mannelli. Such Neapolitan soldiers as did not wish to join him were allowed to make their own way home.

Garibaldi was now only 200 miles from Naples, and he was anxious to get there before Cavour could prevent him from seizing the city in the name of Victor Emmanuel. In spite of the critical situation, King Francis was still unable to act decisively, though after the fall of Palermo he had granted a liberal constitution. The real power now lay in the hands of his minister of the interior, Liborio Romano, who was also chief of police — and he was already negotiating with the Garibaldini to betray the king.

Francis now decided to set up a line of defence between Gaeta and Capua. He had reason to hope that the peasants, who were better off than their cousins in Sicily and Calabria, would remain loyal to him. On September 5 he left Naples and retired, without his government, to Gaeta. He never saw Naples again.

Travelling in an open carriage, Garibaldi continued to make lightning progress up the peninsula, accompanied by just a small force — and a few English visitors, who found this an exciting experience! He reached Salerno, thirty-five miles south of Naples, on the same day as Francis left for Gaeta. He met with a rousing welcome and was told that he could expect a similar one in Naples. 'Naples awaits your arrival with the keenest impatience,' Liborio had assured him in his telegram.

Although he was strongly urged to delay, Garibaldi decided to take the quickest way into the city and on September 7, still accompanied by his English followers, he set off in a special train.

He arrived in Naples soon after midday and travelled to the centre of the city in a carriage. Hundreds of thousands of Neapolitans turned out to cheer him. A route had been chosen to avoid any danger spots but, because of the crowds, his carriage passed along a street which exposed him to the guns of Fort Carmine. Garibaldi was quite unconcerned when warned of the danger.

"Cannons? What cannons?" he retorted. "There are no cannons when the people receive you like this!"

Afterwards he paid a token visit to the cathedral and also made a speech, in which he thanked the people of Naples — diplomatically but quite falsely — for the help they had given in unifying Italy. There were also several appearances from the balcony of his room in the annexe to the palace. The celebrations continued late into the night, long after Garibaldi, now appointed Dictator of the Two Sicilies in the name of King Victor Emmanuel, had retreated to bed.

Garibaldi ruled Naples for two months, from September 7 to November 8, before formally handing over power to Victor Emmanuel. During this time he introduced a number of social and educational reforms, though few of these were allowed to survive his departure. They seemed too radical, setting Naples on the slippery path to socialism. Yet the government he appointed was more conservative than revolutionary, and even Liborio Romano was retained as minister of the interior.

Perhaps what most worried Cavour, waiting anxiously in Turin, was the appointment of Bertani as secretary-general to Garibaldi.

Bertani was a diehard republican, close to Mazzini, who was also living in Naples, though he took no active part in affairs.

Cavour was afraid that Garibaldi, whose loyalty to the king could not be doubted, might be persuaded to delay handing over Naples indefinitely, or at least postpone it until Rome and Venice could be liberated.

Garibaldi still declined to hold a plebiscite, which would allow Naples and Sicily to be annexed to Piedmont. However, he did hand over the whole of the powerful navy, which considerably weakened the independent position that he was trying hard to maintain.

Cavour then came up with his own bold move. He convinced Louis Napoleon that the best way to stop Garibaldi attacking Rome, where the French still maintained a garrison, was to let the Piedmontese army itself invade the Papal States. This would then make its way into the Kingdom of Naples, by-passing Rome, which he guaranteed would not be touched. Louis Napoleon agreed. Like Cavour, he felt sure that Garibaldi did not want a confrontation with the king.

So, on September 11, the Piedmontese under General Fanti invaded the Papal States. The papal troops put up a strong resistance but they were defeated at Perugia, Spoleto and Castelfidardo and by the end of September they had all been forced to surrender at Ancona. The king could now lead his army further south to receive his new kingdom.

In the meantime Garibaldi had fought and won a major battle against King Francis, who, after retreating to Gaeta, had drawn up his army along a twenty-mile front on the River Volturno, which provided a natural line of defence. Against the 50,000-strong Neapolitan army (reinforced with soldiers from Naples who had declined to join the volunteers) Garibaldi could put less than half that number in the field.

All the same it was a much larger army than he had ever commanded before and the circumstances in which he was being forced to fight were very different from those in which he had won his famous victories in the past. Once again, however, he demonstrated his great military ability.

The campaign opened badly with a defeat — the only one Garibaldi suffered during the liberation of the south. This happened while he was away on a brief visit to Sicily, trying to resolve problems that had arisen there in connection with a plebiscite to decide the future of the island.

Türr, one of his commanders, made a rash attack on the Neapolitans at Capua and Caiazzo and suffered heavy casualties. This small victory greatly encouraged the Neapolitans, who started their main offensive in the early hours of October 1.

Forced to fight a largely defensive battle on an extended front, Garibaldi was not always in a position to give his volunteers the kind of personal encouragement which in the past had so often led to victory, though he did lead a number of charges personally. The battle dragged on for two days but, at the end of the first day, Garibaldi had cut off a large enemy force which was very close to capturing Caserta, where he had his headquarters. The following day, with the help of reinforcements from Naples, he was able to drive home his advantage and the enemy surrendered.

His losses were heavier than those of the enemy — over 300 dead and 1300 wounded, which later presented serious problems for the hospitals in Naples. But, although he was in no position to inflict a decisive defeat on the Neapolitans or to attack Rome (as Mazzini would have liked), Naples at least was safe until Victor Emmanuel arrived.

Victor Emmanuel had personally taken command of the Piedmont forces on October 11 and Garibaldi was now ready to hand over to him. However, the annexation of Naples and Sicily to Piedmont had yet to take place. It could be done either through a simple referendum, like the one used in Savoy and Nice earlier in the year, or the citizens could be asked to elect an assembly which would then debate and decide the matter.

Cavour and his representatives in the south preferred the quick solution, which they felt sure would favour Piedmont. The republicans, on the other hand, held out for an elected assembly. Both sides put Garibaldi under a great deal of pressure and both were dissatisfied with him as he swung from one decision to another. A plebiscite in Naples was finally held on October 21 and one in Sicily a week later, with overwhelming majorities in both places in favour of annexation.

On October 25, four days after the plebiscite, Garibaldi rode out of Naples to meet the king. He may well have been feeling a little apprehensive: he had always got on well with Victor Emmanuel, but during the dispute with Cavour, he had written to ask the king to dismiss his prime minister and Victor Emmanuel, not surprisingly, had refused. However, the meeting that took place the following morning near Teano was cordial.

"How are you, my dear Garibaldi?" the king asked.

"Well, Your Majesty. And you?"

"Very well."

85

The two men shook hands and Garibaldi called on his troops to greet 'the first king of Italy'. Then the king and Garibaldi rode off together, talking casually as they went. Later Garibaldi was hurt to learn that the Piedmontese army would be taking over from his volunteers, who were to be sent to the rear.

The Garibaldini were never told, however, that the orders they received from then on came not from him but another commander. The fall of Capua a few days later left Garibaldi angry that he had not been allowed to take it. Gaeta held out until the following spring.

Over the next two weeks Garibaldi was humiliated both by the king's army staff, especially Fanti, and by Farini, who had been sent to take over the administration of Naples. Fanti despised the volunteers. On one occasion, when the king was supposed to go to inspect them at Caserta, he failed to turn up without any explanation — and it has been suggested that he was persuaded by Fanti not to go. Incidents such as this were not forgotten or forgiven by Garibaldi.

The king entered Naples on November 7. Garibaldi was asked to ride at his side in the same carriage — a move, the Mazzinians suggested, to increase the king's popularity. It was raining hard and both men looked depressed. The king in any case did not like formal occasions and never took to his Neapolitan subjects. The following day Garibaldi formally handed over power.

Although the farewell meeting was friendly, Garibaldi refused all the honours that were offered to him — an appointment as general in the Piedmont army, a pension, lands, even a castle and a steamship! He would have liked to be made governor of the south, but this was not an appointment the government in Turin was prepared to make. Instead it was given to Farini, who despised the southerners he was appointed to govern.

Garibaldi left Naples for Caprera on November 9, taking with him only a bag of seed-corn and a few luxury items such as coffee and sugar. The day before he had called on Admiral Mundy, the British commander, to say goodbye and had invited him to visit him on his island. Mundy had said that he would not be free for at least a year and a half. "Well, by that time I won't be on Caprera," Garibaldi had told him. Apparently he expected to be back on the mainland, fighting to free the rest of Italy.

As he sailed out of the harbour at dawn the following day, the guns of the British fleet fired a salute in his honour. Those of the Piedmontese navy remained silent.

20
The Rebel

Small thanks he'd got for nearly doubling the number of the king's subjects!

Of course they'd tried to buy him off with a castle and a steamship, just as they'd bought off the others, Bixio and Medici, with generals' uniforms.

They were the ones who should be helping their fellow-volunteers. Instead they'd gone over to the establishment.

They were all trying to forget the ones who'd done their dirty work, while places were being found in the army for the Bourbons.

But he hadn't forgotten. He'd spoken up for them in parliament. And too bad if that old fox Cavour had suffered for it. His hands had been dirty . . . no doubt about that.

But now the time for action had come again! They hadn't forgotten him down there in the south, where they hated their new masters. He had only to raise the flag and they'd join him in their thousands.

And then the long march towards Naples could begin once more. Only this time it would not stop there. This time it would be Rome . . . or he'd die for it!

Back on Caprera, Garibaldi derived a great deal of satisfaction from his self-chosen life as a simple 'farmer', as he described himself in the census returns.

He woke early and, long before daybreak, had dealt with his correspondence, which arrived by the sackful from his many admirers all over the world. Then, after a cup of coffee, he worked first in the kitchen garden, where he grew vegetables for his family, and later for much of the day in the fields and the vineyards.

There was always plenty to be done: the poor soil needed attention; rocks had to be broken up and walls had to be mended to keep out his neighbour's goats. When work was over for the day, he could relax with his favourite pastimes — hunting and fishing.

Nor was he lonely on the island. He had most of his family about him. Teresita was there, now an attractive young girl and already married to one of his officers, Major Canzio, and so was Menotti, who had served with his father on the Sicilian expedition. Later they were joined by Ricciotti, who had been at school in England. He had become so English that Garibaldi jokingly protested that he had difficulty communicating with him.

Garibaldi had also brought back two of his horses, Marsala and Calatefimi, from the war, and had a number of donkeys named after his favourite enemies — Pius IX, Franz Josef and Louis Napoleon. He was greatly attached to all his animals.

There were numerous visitors and guests too. Some, such as Guerzoni, who worked as his secretary and later wrote his biography, stayed permanently or for long periods. Old friends such as Vecchi came and went.

Then there were the admirers, who also came in large numbers. Many of these stayed on La Maddalena and would come across to meet the great man. Most visitors carried a souvenir away with them: if they were lucky, a lock of his hair, which was in great demand from the ladies, or at the very least an autograph.

The house itself was far from comfortable and still not well furnished. Garibaldi's own room was damp because it was over the well, and was always untidy, littered with his papers and newspapers — and with his washing, which he usually did for himself.

Food was simple but plentiful. Garibaldi himself ate little meat and preferred milk or water to wine. The evening meal was a ceremonial occasion, with Garibaldi at the head of the table. If the general was in a good mood, it would end with stories from his past, with singing his favourite songs, and perhaps even some dancing.

Sometimes, however, perhaps brooding on events, Garibaldi would sit in moody silence and then retire abruptly to bed. At all events, whatever his family and guests did, he always went to bed early.

But Garibaldi still kept in close contact with the outside world and expected at any time to be called back to the mainland to continue the struggle for the liberation of the rest of Italy. He had not forgotten the part he had played in making Italy and the fact that he had almost doubled the number of Victor Emmanuel's subjects.

Already there was trouble in the south, which was being badly administered. He was reluctant to intervene but, when he finally agreed to stand for parliament in the election held early in 1861, it is significant that he became a deputy for Naples.

However, the news that disturbed him most was the treatment of his volunteers. Most of the original 'Thousand' had been absorbed into the regular army, and his leading commanders, such as Bixio, Medici, Cosenz and Türr had been made generals (perhaps to win them over to Cavour). Many others, however, simply could not be taken in, especially since places had to be found for officers from the regular Bourbon army.

To some it even seemed that the enemy was getting preferential treatment. Garibaldi, no doubt urged on by politicians anxious to undermine Cavour, felt that he had to do something for the men who had contributed so much to the liberation of the south. In April 1861 he decided to go to Turin to take his seat in parliament. He had already decided that Cavour was to blame for everything!

He appeared in the chamber on April 20. The visitors' gallery was packed. Dressed in a poncho and a red shirt, he was sworn in as a deputy and took his seat. From statements he had already made, it was thought that he was going to ask for a volunteer army to be formed, instead of attacking Cavour for the government's treatment of the volunteers.

After a long dull speech by General Fanti, defending the government's handling of the problem, Garibaldi suddenly accused Cavour of having planned to attack the Garibaldini when the Piedmontese army invaded the Papal States the previous autumn. An uproar broke out and Cavour lost his temper; but Garibaldi refused to withdraw his accusation. In the pandemonium that followed, the session had to be abandoned for a while.

In spite of a conciliatory speech by Cavour, Garibaldi persisted in his attacks and also in his call for the formation of a separate army of volunteers. Then, amid cheers, he abruptly left the chamber. But the vote went against him, with the house heavily in favour of the government's army policy.

The row between Cavour and Garibaldi smouldered on. Then the king intervened. He called Cavour and Garibaldi to the palace and asked them to shake hands. The two men spoke in a friendly way — but did not shake hands. "I never saw his hands," Cavour said. "He held them all the time under his prophet's mantle!"

Less than a month later Cavour died of a sudden illness. It was even suggested that the quarrel with Garibaldi had helped to kill him, although in the meantime the two men had exchanged cordial letters.

For a while Garibaldi, back on Caprera, seemed interested in going to the United States to fight on the side of the north in the American Civil War. The prospect of fighting a war to free the slaves appealed to his romantic temperament. But he wanted the command of the entire army and a commitment that all the slaves would be freed, and this was not a guarantee the authorities were prepared to give a foreigner.

Meanwhile there were plenty of rumours as to where he would strike next. Venice was a likely target, since the French still protected the Pope in Rome — but might not oppose an attack which would weaken the Austrians. But it was probable that any attack would be indirect, perhaps by stirring up trouble in Dalmatia. Garibaldi was clearly the right man for such an enterprise and could be trusted to keep quiet about any government involvement.

There was, unquestionably, close contact between Garibaldi, on the one hand, and the king and his new prime minister, the wily Rattazzi, on the other hand. In the spring of 1862, Garibaldi toured many of the cities in the north of Italy, making rousing speeches and calling on the people to practise rifle-shooting in their spare time. He was cheered wherever he went and from the receptions held in his honour, it might be concluded that his tour was official.

At some point, however, the government, or at least Rattazzi, became alarmed, and even more so when Garibaldi held a secret meeting at Trescore on May 5 (the second anniversary of the sailing of the Thousand from Quarto) with his leading officers and discussed plans with them for taking Venice by means of an invasion of Dalmatia.

He had been promised money, he assured them; a million lire. Many, especially the Mazzinians, opposed the idea, perhaps because it had official support, but some wanted to go ahead. Shortly afterwards, on May 15, Colonel Nullo, one of Garibaldi's leading officers, was arrested at Sarnico together with about a hundred volunteers. A few days later some were shot while trying to escape.

Garibaldi was furious and denounced the government, both in a funeral speech and in an open letter to parliament. He had been called from Caprera, he protested; he had been promised money and arms. Rattazzi tried to cover up. He admitted that Garibaldi had been promised money, but not for an attack on Austria.

Once again Garibaldi retreated to Caprera. The volunteers who had been arrested were released and there was no parliamentary inquiry into the incident. Government involvement could not be doubted. Even Cavour, it later emerged, had been plotting along the same lines before his death, smuggling large quantities of arms into the Balkans.

Not long afterwards, at the end of June 1862, Garibaldi left

Caprera again. This time it was for Sicily — 'for the unknown', as he chose to put it.

His intentions at this stage are not clear. Doubtless he was interested in revisiting the scenes of his former glory. Possibly even then he had visions of repeating his triumphant march up through the peninsula — except that this time he did not intend to stop at Naples. Perhaps in all this he had the secret support of the king. At any rate he carried with him a mysterious document with a red seal . . . and it was soon evident that he was not short of money.

Shortly after he landed at Palermo, where his speeches were received with wild acclaim, there were shouts for Rome and Venice. Then, as he toured the provinces and came to Marsala, the cry of 'Rome or death!' began to be heard. With drawn sword Garibaldi swore an oath 'Rome or death!' in the cathedral — and soon the cry of 'Rome or death!' could be heard everywhere.

Volunteers, a great many of them hungry and in rags, swarmed in to join him and in a short time there were 3000 of them, all clamouring for action. Some of his former officers came to join him, though others warned him to be careful of the consequences. Even if he had not intended to invade the mainland, there was no turning back now.

Once again Rattazzi became alarmed as the volunteer army marched towards Catania, where the regular troops did nothing to stop his progress. The navy had been given ambiguous instructions: 'Do anything the occasion demands, but always keep in mind your King and country.'

In the event, they kept out of the way while Garibaldi made further preparations. On August 24 he seized two merchant ships and crossed to Calabria, landing once again at Melito.

This time, however, there was to be no triumphant progress up the peninsula . . .

By now Rattazzi had already decided that firm action was called for. Louis Napoleon had rejected his proposal that the Piedmontese should be allowed to occupy Rome in order to defend it from Garibaldi and so Rattazzi was forced to send an army to the south. Its commander was General Cialdini, who disliked Garibaldi and was only too anxious to have the opportunity to fight him.

Garibaldi had already declined to clash with the garrison at Reggio. He headed into the mountains and in doing so got lost, going round in almost a complete circle and ending up near Aspromonte. His men were wet and hungry; they had had little to eat except for some raw potatoes. Many of his volunteers now began to desert.

At this point, on August 29, the Piedmontese troops, under Colonel Pallavicini, caught up with him. His orders were 'to pursue Garibaldi constantly without giving him a moment's rest. Attack him if he seeks to escape and destroy him if he accepts battle.'

Garibaldi stationed his men in a very secure position, but he did not want to engage in battle against his fellow-Italians. Nor did he seriously believe that they would want to engage in battle with him. As the Piedmontese advanced, he told his men to hold their fire, even though the other side were firing on them. Unfortunately some of his volunteers began to fire back. "Don't fire!" Garibaldi kept repeating. At this point he clutched his thigh and fell wounded to the ground. There seems little doubt that the well-known figure of the general was a specific target.

When the doctor examined him, he was found to be badly wounded in the foot. "Amputate it if you have to!" Garibaldi told him, puffing away on his cigar.

Meanwhile, after the firing had stopped, an officer rode up and demanded his surrender. Garibaldi had him disarmed for his discourteous behaviour. In the end Colonel Pallavicini came in person. "I have to perform a very unpleasant duty," he said apologetically as he asked for unconditional surrender.

There followed a painful fifteen-hour journey on a stretcher down the mountainside. He was put on board a ship, the *Duca di Genova*, and taken off to Varignano, near Spezia, where he was put in prison.

There were some in authority who would have liked to see him put on trial — even if he was reprieved immediately afterwards. But the matter could not be too deeply investigated because Rattazzi was clearly implicated and even the king had to admit that he had encouraged Garibaldi 'to some extent'. Perhaps this was why some attempt had been made to kill him. In the end, he and his volunteers were pardoned, except for those who had deserted from the army. Some of these were shot. For Pallavicini and the men who had captured him, on the other hand, medals were given liberally.

Garibaldi's wound gave him a good deal of trouble, though it also aroused sympathy for him all over the world. Doctors came from all over Europe to offer advice, and in England, where he seemed like a martyr, money was raised to pay for his treatment. Telegrams, letters, flowers, books . . . presents of all description flooded in for the sick hero.

The bullet was finally extracted by a Tuscan surgeon, Professor Zanetti, and was kept as a souvenir by Menotti. A month later Garibaldi was allowed to return to Caprera. There was little risk that he would get up to any similar escapade for some time to come.

21
The Idol

It had, he supposed, been vanity on his part to come to England in the first place. But innocent enough.

He'd been looking forward to a little flattery — crowds lining the streets, bands playing and a few receptions.

And crowds there had been . . . half London must have turned out to see him. There hadn't been anything like this since Sicily and Naples!

But why must they spoil it all by fighting over his favours — these English 'milords' and Mazzini and his friends?

He'd given his word: no politics . . . and this time he meant it. But that didn't rule out an evening or two with one's old mates, surely? Some of them were down on their luck these days.

But these aristocrats had tried from the start to fence him in. They'd dreamt up an endless round of engagements, hoping that way he'd have no time for mischief.

While their ladies, on their side, tried to tempt him into other mischief! But he'd keep quiet about that. They were welcome to their 'souvenirs' — his hair and bottled bathwater! Though he sometimes wondered what they did with it all . . .

It was a pity, in the end, it had turned out so disappointing. But, frankly, he wouldn't be sorry to get back to his own island . . . and a good night's sleep!

After over a year on Caprera, which he spent hobbling around on crutches while he recovered from his wound at Aspromonte, Garibaldi finally agreed to visit England in April 1864.

Like many of his ventures, a good deal of mystery hangs over the visit. It is not entirely clear why he went in the first place and why he then cut short his visit and left so abruptly. His own statements made at the time were contradictory and he makes no mention of the visit in his memoirs. It is almost as if, in the end, he preferred to draw a veil over this fourth and final visit to a country which he greatly admired and where he was himself the object of great affection.

He arrived at the port of Southampton on the evening of April 3 on board the liner *Ripon*, which he had caught at Malta. He was accompanied by both his sons, Menotti and Ricciotti, as well as his secretaries and his personal doctor.

In spite of the rain, huge crowds turned out to see the hero of Sicily, whose image was now deeply rooted in the popular imagination. There was the first of many receptions in his honour, and Garibaldi made a speech in his very limited English. The following day he was taken to the Isle of Wight, where, for the next week, he was the guest of the Liberal MP Charles Seely.

To Mazzini and his English radical friends, who had been hoping to be in control of Garibaldi's visit in order to organise rallies and raise money (probably for an attack on Venice), it was a great blow to find him so firmly in the hands of their aristocratic opponents — who, on their side, were equally determined not to let him fall into the hands of the revolutionaries.

Politically the visit had caused some concern from the start but Garibaldi himself had already made it clear that he did not want to be the cause of 'political demonstrations and disturbances'. Publicly at least he stated that he had come to see his English friends. Perhaps at this stage he hoped somehow to keep both sides happy — as he had so often done in the past.

But at any rate, during his stay on the Isle of Wight, his radical friends were not denied access to him, as they were afraid they might be. Mazzini came twice, as well as the Russian revolutionary in exile, Alexander Herzen, who later wrote a book about Garibaldi's visit. Other associates of Mazzini also had no difficulty in getting to see him.

At the same time he was kept busy with engagements on a different level. Lord Shaftesbury came to see him — hoping that he might find in Garibaldi a true Protestant and not just an opponent of the Pope — and also the Poet Laureate, Lord Tennyson. Tennyson invited him to his house and later wrote some verses about the tree which 'the warrior of Caprera' planted. There was also a visit to inspect the dockyards at Portsmouth.

Then, on April 11, a special train was arranged to take him to London. His aristocratic admirers were determined to make this the centre of his visit. His radical friends, no less stubbornly, were pressing him to spend his time in the provinces.

By now a kind of 'Garibaldi-mania' was sweeping the country. The ladies were fashionably dressed in Garibaldi blouses and hats; biscuits had been named in his honour and Garibaldi songs were being sung in music halls. People turned out in their thousands along the route to see his train pass and to call out "God bless you, Garibaldi!"

But this was nothing to the popular reception that awaited him from the time he entered the outskirts of London. There at least half a million people lined the streets as the Duke of Sutherland's carriage took him to Stafford House, where he was to stay for most of the time he was in London. There were representatives from working-class organisations from all over the country, with banners, bands and cheering all along the route.

But, it was noted, the occasion was completely orderly: no one was drunk and no arrests were made by the police, who kept in the background. However, in the course of the three-mile journey, which took several hours to complete, so many people pressed against the side of the carriage that it later fell to pieces.

Mazzini's worst suspicions were, however, soon confirmed: Garibaldi had let himself be taken over by the establishment. Not only was Garibaldi's entourage excluded from Stafford House (where the servants were busy bottling and selling the water the general had washed in), but for the next two weeks Garibaldi himself was treated as if he were a visiting monarch.

The very next day he had lunch with the Prime Minister, Lord Palmerston, whose conservative views were unlikely to coincide with his own. Indeed, after their private talk, Garibaldi is reported to have come away with a red face. He had been asked by Palmerston, it seems, not to start another war over Venice. Garibaldi was not pleased to be asked to delay the liberation of a part of Italy. In his opinion it was never too soon to break the chains of slaves.

In the course of his stay he became the darling of society ladies, and more than one appears to have fallen in love with him, and later wrote him indiscreet letters, which he replied to rather formally. There were visits to the House of Lords; to the opera; to the Crystal Palace . . . as well as endless dinners and receptions. He was also given the freedom of the City of London. But on one occasion at least his own sons were not admitted to a dinner in his honour because they were wearing the wrong clothes.

Such a life was the reverse of his usual simple routine of early nights and it is not surprising that he soon began to look tired and the news got around that he was not well.

Nor did his visit meet with favour in all quarters. Queen Victoria strongly disapproved of the frivolous behaviour of her subjects and was 'half-ashamed of being head of a nation capable of such follies'. For her he was a revolutionary leader who wanted to attack the

Austrians and who favoured the cause of Denmark against the Germans. She was not personally impressed with Garibaldi's own admiration for the way she ruled England, which he declared was almost like a republic.

Her son, however, the Prince of Wales (and the future King Edward VII), did go to see Garibaldi against his mother's wishes and was suitably impressed. He found him 'dignified and noble'. Among the politicians, Disraeli refused to meet him and Karl Marx, who detested Mazzini, called the visit a 'miserable spectacle of imbecility'.

The French, on the other hand, were alarmed by the success of the visit and suspected Garibaldi's intentions. However, they contented themselves with observing, sourly but perhaps accurately, that Garibaldi would get plenty of entertainment in England — 'plum pudding and turtle soup' — but 'no money for muskets', if that was what he had really come for.

In Italy the visit had caused annoyance from the start and the Italian diplomatic mission had been ordered to boycott all receptions in his honour. Even at the height of his popularity, Garibaldi had never been fêted in this way in his own country and it was felt perhaps that this kind of royal treatment might give him ideas of grandeur.

In England the main protests came from the Catholics and the Irish, but concern in government circles grew when it was learnt that he had accepted invitations to visit a large number of cities in the provinces. This, it was felt, was bound to result in agitation and disorder.

Yet, in spite of his crowded programme of receptions, Garibaldi still found time for a visit to Herzen's house on the outskirts of London, to which he travelled in his host's carriage, and at a meal there he paid a moving and generous tribute to Mazzini.

"There is a man amongst us who has rendered the greatest service to our country and to the cause of freedom," he said. "When I was young I looked for someone to act as the guide and counsellor of my youthful years . . . This man is Giuseppe Mazzini — my friend and teacher."

It was all too much for Mazzini. He took Garibaldi's hand after the toast in his honour and murmured: "*E troppo!*" (It's more than I deserve!)

Official circles were alarmed by Garibaldi's mixing with radicals and revolutionaries on what was supposed to be a private visit — though they should not have been surprised. Garibaldi was a generous-minded man and had already told Lord Shaftesbury that he could not turn his back on Mazzini. "If I had found him in prosperity," he said, "I would have avoided all misunderstanding by not seeing him; but finding him in adversity I could not throw him aside."

Soon afterwards, on April 18, it was announced that General Garibaldi would shortly be concluding his visit and would therefore not be going to the provinces after all. It was said that the visit had been too much for him, and that he was ill and exhausted.

His own doctor disagreed but Garibaldi at the time declined to comment openly, beyond saying that he would not stay where he was not wanted. It was widely believed, however, that Gladstone may have been responsible for his abrupt departure.

Gladstone had been given the task of asking Garibaldi not to take on his provincial tour and, failing perhaps to express himself clearly in Italian, had given Garibaldi the impression that he was 'not wanted'.

After a few more receptions, at one of which the exhausted Garibaldi remained seated while he greeted an endless stream of admirers, and a quick visit to Eton, where he was wildly cheered, it was arranged that he should leave on the Duke of Sutherland's yacht. The duke, it seems, was hoping to take him further than Caprera — perhaps to the Middle East, which would have effectively kept him out of mischief for a while.

At all events, on April 22 Garibaldi left London. "I shall be happy to return under more fortunate circumstances," he declared. "For the moment I am obliged to leave England."

He had one more visit to fit in — to go to Cornwall to see Colonel Peard, who had fought with him in Calabria in 1860. Again there were crowds along the route and receptions at Exeter and Plymouth. He finally sailed on April 28. Queen Victoria at least was glad to see the back of him. 'Garibaldi, thank God, is gone!' she wrote.

Despite the duke's pressing invitation to go on a long cruise, Garibaldi asked to be taken straight back to Caprera. There may even have been a scheme afoot to involve him in an attack on Austria, since shortly afterwards he left for Ischia, where some of the time at least was spent in meetings.

But there can be no doubt that for everyone the visit had not turned out as well as it had been hoped. Mazzini and his friends had failed to get the use of him for popular demonstrations in the provinces, while his aristocratic admirers had in the end exhausted him with their attentions. His own entourage, accommodated in a cheap hotel, and often denied access to the celebrations in his honour, must have been dissatisfied with their treatment.

Garibaldi himself tried to keep the peace by leaving quietly and later wrote a letter to the press, denying that he had been forced to leave. After that he made no further public statement.

22
The Dreamer

So here he was, after all these years, once more at Monte Rotondo! But this time he was advancing on Rome, not running away. Although then he'd called it 'retreating' . . . !

In all those years the dream had never faded. Rome, one day, would be the capital of a free and united Italy. And now he was within a stone's throw of the city.

And it wasn't just his dream now . . . there were others who shared it. Who knew in their hearts that the true capital couldn't be elsewhere. But they left it to him to translate thought into action.

If only he had his Roman troops behind him now! He'd grumbled then, but at least they were battle-hardened. These new ones were too raw and whined all the time about comfort. Did they expect three meals a day and a soft bed to lie on?

Still, he'd already given the Pope's soldiers a taste of what to expect. Three hours of fighting — and they'd been glad to surrender. And glad too to accept the rations of bread and water he'd given them. "Long live Garibaldi!" they'd all shouted.

Next stop Mentana, then! It had to be now or never!

And if he failed, he'd give up his dream for ever!

In September 1864 France and Italy signed a pact over Rome. The French agreed to withdraw their troops, and the Italians undertook not only to defend the Pope but also to move the capital from Turin to Florence. The agreement was intended to prevent any further attempts on Rome.

But Venice was still a legitimate target and it was felt that, with Trieste and the Tyrol in Austrian hands, Italy's frontiers still remained exposed to attack. The army too longed for a chance to prove its worth in battle: so far the territories that made up the new Italy had been the gift of France and Garibaldi or the result of voluntary accession.

The opportunity to gain Venice was offered by Prussia, who was looking for an ally in a war against Austria. Italy, anxious to expand her territory and to secure her frontiers, seemed the obvious choice and a secret alliance was formed. The military, led by General La Marmora, who was also prime minister at the time, and by Cialdini, favoured a direct attack on Venice in order to demonstrate Italy's fighting ability.

In the build-up to the war, Austria even offered to give up Venice but the offer was scornfully dismissed. This time the Italians felt capable of defeating their old enemy, and, besides, they wanted Trieste and the Tyrol.

In any war against Venice a role had to be found for Garibaldi, although he was kept in the background on Caprera for as long as possible. At one stage it was proposed, perhaps by the king, that he and his volunteers should land in Dalmatia to fight a guerrilla war behind enemy lines.

The Prussians approved, as did Garibaldi himself. He liked the idea of an independent command. But La Marmora vetoed the scheme: he wanted to fight a straight war against the Austrians. So, when Garibaldi was eventually brought across from Caprera in mid-June 1866, he was put in charge of the campaign in the Tyrol.

He established his headquarters at Salò on Lake Garda and immediately threw himself into the difficult task of turning his volunteers into a fighting force, capable of fighting a guerrilla-type war in the mountains.

He had to face the same old problems: antiquated rifles, inferior equipment and inadequate medical supplies. But at least his men were allowed to wear their red shirts, perhaps to save the cost of uniforms. The total force of volunteers — a mixed lot as usual — numbered over thirty thousand, although half of these were kept in the south of Italy, perhaps to prevent Garibaldi from becoming too powerful.

Meanwhile the main Italian army, which was superior in numbers to the Austrians, had been extended over a wide front. The two commanders, La Marmora and Cialdini — who were jealous of each other as well as of Garibaldi — failed to work together and part of the army was soon defeated at Custoza in a minor engagement with the Austrians.

Then, to the surprise of the Austrians, La Marmora ordered the Italians to retreat thirty miles and so demoralised his troops. Garibaldi was ordered to protect the retreating army but he was soon back in the Tyrol, fighting a campaign over difficult ground.

"Be eagles!" he told his volunteers, as they fought their way from one mountain top to another. Crippled with rheumatism and suffering from a wound in the thigh, he was obliged to direct operations from a carriage. But he won the only significant victory of the war when he defeated the Austrians at Bezzecca, though with losses of over two thousand men.

Then came news of another disaster: the Italian navy had been disgracefully defeated at Lissa, despite the fact that they greatly outnumbered the enemy. At this point the Prussians, who had defeated the Austrians at Sadowa, decided to call an end to the war and the Italians had no option but to do the same.

Garibaldi, meanwhile, had pressed on far into the Tyrol and was in sight of Trento, which he might have captured. With victory within his reach, he was ordered to retreat. "I obey," was his laconic response to these unwelcome instructions.

Fifty years later, a war lasting three years was fought for Trento — and over half a million Italians lost their lives.

In the negotiations that followed, Italy gained Venice — but Austria, who had won two victories, refused to hand it over directly. Instead, it was given to France, who in turn passed it on to Italy — just like 'secondhand goods'. A senseless war had been fought for what might have been gained for nothing. And, with Trieste and the Tyrol still firmly in the hands of the Austrians, the frontiers of Italy were just as exposed as ever.

Garibaldi and his volunteers went home in a bitter mood: they had fought a tough campaign with no support — not even from the peasants they were supposed to be liberating — and then at the last moment they had been deprived of their goal.

In spite of the agreement with France, Garibaldi clung obstinately to his belief that Rome could and should be liberated and become once more the capital of Italy. It was his boyhood dream and his obsession seemed to increase as he grew older. He was now nearing sixty and perhaps he felt that time was running out.

Thus, during an election campaign early in 1867, he increased his attacks on the Pope, who had recently published a 'Syllabus of Errors', condemning all progressive ideas. Garibaldi campaigned for a government that would make a fresh start . . . that would wipe out the defeats of Custoza and Lissa by taking Rome.

Some Italian politicians, who disliked having the capital at Florence, also felt that a solution to the problem had to be found — perhaps by stirring up trouble in the Papal States, which would provide an excuse to send in the army to restore order. There was government connivance when Garibaldi, together with Menotti and Ricciotti, began to collect funds and recruit volunteers — who, on his instructions, openly wore red shirts and carried arms.

But Garibaldi was going ahead too fast or perhaps too openly and the order went out to put a stop to these goings on. It was too late: "How can we arrest an entire population?" one official protested.

Preparations for an invasion of the Papal States did not prevent Garibaldi from paying a hurried visit to Geneva to attend an International Congress for Peace, which was being attended by many famous people. Ideas dear to Garibaldi's heart were to be discussed: the need to give up war and settle disputes through arbitration.

He gave a moderate speech but the programme he subsequently proposed — which included abolishing the papacy — took many by surprise. Garibaldi himself, however, did not stay to listen to the agitated discussion that followed. At that point he was more interested in actions than in words.

Back in Florence, he continued with his plans for an attack on Rome. The government was involved, but Rattazzi, once again prime minister, could not declare himself openly. On his side, however, Garibaldi certainly expected to be able to count on government support. He thought that 'a few shots in the air' would be enough to start a revolution in Rome — and then the Italian army would march in to support him.

When he moved south towards the papal frontier, however, Rattazzi had him arrested. He was put in gaol in Alessandria and, to cut short the wave of protests that followed, he was sent back to Caprera. There, for the next few weeks, he was blockaded on the island by nine warships of the Italian navy. It was perhaps a gesture to keep the European powers quiet, especially the French, though all the while, it seems, help was still being given to the volunteers, commanded at the time by Menotti.

Garibaldi himself was determined not to be left out of this attack on Rome. Already, in October, there had been several raids across the frontier into papal territory. Twice he tried to escape, once even travelling on the steamer as far as Genoa. Finally he managed to get away in a small boat, disguised as a fisherman and with his beard dyed black.

Two days later Garibaldi reached Livorno and on October 20 he was back in Florence, where he made a provocative speech. "Italy expects every man to do his duty!" he thundered. No move was made to arrest Garibaldi and Louis Napoleon announced that he was sending an expeditionary force to protect the Pope. The French kept a battalion at Toulon, ready to sail to Rome at a moment's notice.

Victor Emmanuel now ordered Garibaldi's arrest, perhaps to cover up his own involvement. Rattazzi resigned and for several days the king had difficulty finding a prime minister to replace him. Meantime, however, Garibaldi had gone south to join Menotti at Monte Rotondo, where the papal forces had just been defeated. The following day the city itself was stormed and taken.

But in Rome a revolt to support the Garibaldini had broken out and failed. Little attempt had been made to keep the plans secret and it was easily put down by the gendarmes, helped by a thunderstorm which scattered the revolutionaries. The Garibaldini, led by the Cairoli brothers, made a bold attempt to get into the city but this too ended in disaster.

Nor was this war to liberate Rome in any way a happy affair. The weather was bad and the volunteers were short of food. As usual, there was no support from the peasants. With news of the failed revolt in Rome and the arrival of the French troops at Civitavecchia, desertions increased by the day.

Then the new prime minister, General Menabrea, announced that he was sending an army to help the French. Once again, Garibaldi had been disowned and abandoned! But it was too late to turn back. In any case, he believed that, if he could unite all his troops, he stood a chance of defeating the papal and French forces separately.

Garibaldi did not yet know that the French were armed with a new and powerful weapon — a fast-firing rifle.

On November 3 he came into conflict with the papal forces at Mentana. Although outnumbered nearly two to one, the Garibaldini were at one stage on the point of victory. But then 2000 French troops arrived with their superior rifles. The French did not have to advance: they simply fired.

'The unseen enemy descended upon us, thinning our ranks . . . The only sign of them was the death they scattered among us . . .!' The Garibaldini fled; 150 were killed and another 1600 taken prisoner. The French lost only 2 men.

Garibaldi himself managed to escape across the frontier with a few of his men. The Italian army was waiting for them. His men were disarmed and taken back to their homes. Garibaldi himself was arrested at the small railway station of Figline, while he was travelling to Livorno.

But he was not prepared to surrender without a protest. After all, was he not a deputy and, in his own eyes at least, an American citizen (though he had got no further than taking out the papers)? Besides, he demanded, what crime had he committed against the State?

The officer who had been sent to carry out this difficult task listened respectfully. He even contacted Florence for further instructions but, when none came, he went ahead and arrested Garibaldi. He was taken away by four *carabinieri* and once again put in prison in Varignano, where he spent the next three weeks.

Perhaps it was hoped that Garibaldi would say something to involve Rattazzi. In the event he kept silent. He knew that the government would not dare to put him on trial: there would be too much public protest and, in any case, they had too much to hide.

On November 27 1867 he gave his word that he would return to Caprera, and there he remained for the next three years. His dream of making Rome the capital of Italy had finally been shattered.

23
The Ageing Lion

*It had all passed so swiftly . . . and now he was old and worn . . .
fingers so stiff that sometimes he could hardly stir the smoking fire.*

*On good days he could still hobble about his garden, leaning on
Francesca. More often than not, though, she pushed him around in
a wheelchair!*

The hero of two worlds . . . with hardly the strength of a baby!

*Yet, more than ever now, he needed money. The island gobbled it
up like a greedy monster! He'd even tried selling the rock — there
was plenty of that to spare! But in the end it had cost him more than
it brought him.*

*The others had all grown rich, while he'd done all the fighting.
The Pope had been right there . . . they two alone had made
nothing out of the making of Italy!*

*So what was left? Should he turn his hand to writing? Others had
made money that way . . . with no more talent than he had! Besides,
he could tell a good story . . . and had plenty to tell! There were
some who might begin to sleep less well in their beds at night!*

*Perhaps the time had come, then, to lay down the sword . . . and
take up the pen.*

For three years after his defeat at Mentana, Garibaldi was virtually
a prisoner on Caprera. Crippled by rheumatism and troubled by the
wound he had got at Aspromonte, he was ageing rapidly and was no
longer physically active.

Even so, he had to find an outlet for his energy and since his
memoirs had met with great success, he now decided to turn his
hand to writing historical novels. He knew he had no great literary
talent, but he felt he could at least tell a good story. Besides, he
needed the money, as he freely admitted, and he had seen others
grow rich and famous in this way.

When he had finished his first novel — called in Italian *Clelia*,
after his youngest daughter — he decided to ask the opinion of his
old friend, Speranza, who was herself an established writer.

Clelia was the romantic story of four pairs of lovers who, after a series of adventures, all die at Mentana fighting to liberate Rome. It reflected in particular Garibaldi's intense anti-clerical feelings, which he could now relieve only on an imaginative level.

Speranza thought the novel was so bad that she advised him not to publish it, but Garibaldi was determined to go ahead. Over a dozen publishers rejected it but in the end, because of his name, he succeeded in getting it brought out not only in Italian but also in English and German translations. One reviewer described it as 'almost more pitiable than absurd'.

Garibaldi wrote two more historical novels, largely based on his own experiences, but these were not translated. He also wrote a good deal of poetry about the most exciting episodes in his life — from Montevideo to Mentana — which form a kind of autobiography in verse, and he set down his thoughts on the wide range of topics that interested him — such as government, capital punishment and women.

In 1872 he completed the final version of his memoirs. It had already been translated into French by Alexander Dumas, and into German by Speranza. In the final version Garibaldi brought the story up as far as Mentana and his campaign in the Franco-Prussian war. At the same time he sharpened his judgements on a number of prominent people, such as Mazzini and King Victor Emmanuel, and attacked even more violently than before institutions like the Church.

When Speranza came to see Garibaldi on Caprera in the summer of 1868, she met for the first time Francesca Armosino, Garibaldi's latest (and last) mistress. His former housekeeper, Battistina, by whom he had had a daughter, Anita, nearly ten years before, had gone back to Nice, supported by an allowance which Garibaldi made her.

Francesca had first come to Caprera as nurse to one of Teresita's many children and not long afterwards became Garibaldi's mistress — much to the annoyance of Teresita, who quarrelled with her father over the affair and left the island. In 1867 Clelia had been born, and after that there were two more children: Rosa, who died while her father was fighting in France in 1871, and a boy named Manlio.

Speranza thought that Francesca was a 'rough-looking woman' and indeed, like most of Garibaldi's women, she was plain and unattractive and of peasant origin. Garibaldi, however, was not interested in Speranza's opinion of Francesca, who was clearly now the mistress of the household.

Apart from her literary advice, which he did not take, he wanted her help with Battistina and Anita, who were also there on a visit to Caprera. Garibaldi asked Speranza to take charge of his daughter. Speranza agreed to help. Later, when she left the island, she took Anita with her and put her in a boarding school in Switzerland, where she would get a strict education.

But Garibaldi, who was inclined to spoil his children, soon found fault with the school when Anita began to get ideas above her station. Speranza then took Anita to live with her in her house in Crete, where she was treated little better than a servant.

Years later, while he was in Rome in 1875, Garibaldi got a letter from his daughter in an envelope addressed simply to 'General Garibaldi', which she had thrown into the street out of the window of Speranza's house. In it she begged her father to let her come home.

Garibaldi at once sent Menotti to fetch Anita, who was now sixteen years old. She arrived, he wrote in his letter to Speranza, 'well, and already a woman; but with a load of lice more than I have ever seen on any human creature . . . ' Speranza did not reply and from that time on their correspondence ceased.

As for Anita, two months later she fell ill while she was playing one morning on the beach. She had caught meningitis, and a few hours later she was dead.

Garibaldi's last campaign was not for the liberation of Rome, which, in the end, had taken place almost without a struggle.

In the summer of 1870, a war broke out between France and Prussia and in August, Louis Napoleon withdrew his troops from Rome. A month later he was defeated at Sedan and went into exile in England. Victor Emmanuel wasted no time: he announced that he was entering Rome to preserve order in the city. The Pope protested, but it was no use. The Italian army marched into Rome and the people voted to become part of Italy.

Early the following year Rome finally became the official capital when parliament moved there and the king took up his residence. The unity of Italy was now complete — but in the final stage there had been no part for Garibaldi to play. Almost unmoved, he had watched events from Caprera, where warships ensured that he did not leave the island to take part.

When the war between France and Prussia first broke out, Garibaldi had been on the side of Prussia: he hoped that Louis Napoleon would be 'rewarded for his villainies'. When this happened, and France became a republic, at the same time declining to make peace with Prussia, Garibaldi's sympathies changed.

He became an ardent supporter of the new republic and believed all the evil stories that were told about Prussia. "It is Italy's duty to fly to the assistance of France now that Napoleon no longer dishonours her," he announced — and promptly offered his services — 'what is left of me' — to France.

His Garibaldini were embarrassed — and the French no less. "That's all that was needed!" exclaimed one member of the government in despair. However, Garibaldi was determined to join in the war while it lasted, for perhaps he knew that it must be his final one.

When he landed at Marseilles early in October, he was offered at first only a small command — a force of a mere 300 volunteers — which he rejected. After much argument, he was put in command of the so-called 'Army of the Vosges', an international brigade made up of several thousand volunteers. It was the kind of command well suited to his talents.

His two sons, Menotti and Ricciotti, each commanded a brigade and Jessie White Mario came to nurse the wounded. She had not seen Garibaldi since Mentana and she was shocked to discover how much he had aged — 'with his white beard and pale face looking like a soldier with one foot in the grave', as one journalist described him. He could no longer mount a horse without assistance and sometimes he was so ill he had to be carried around on a stretcher.

Yet, despite criticism from the ungrateful French and the inevitable disagreements with other French generals with whom he failed to co-operate, Garibaldi did not disgrace himself and for his own part he regarded the war as one of his most successful campaigns.

The volunteers had to face a well-trained and much larger army. In spite of heavy snow, Ricciotti won an early engagement against 1000 Prussians and took a large number of prisoners. Later, when repelling an attack on Dijon, he also managed to capture the colours of a crack Prussian regiment.

As always, Garibaldi's greatest successes were his rapid skirmishes and the Prussians freely acknowledged that his flying columns hampered their movements. But nothing he did could effect the eventual outcome of the war. An armistice was signed early in 1871 and Garibaldi returned to Caprera.

From now on Garibaldi only left his island for short intervals. In 1875, when he decided to pay his first visit to Rome since 1849, there was some apprehension in official circles. But it turned out that his main concern was a scheme to divert the course of the Tiber to prevent Rome from being flooded every year. The scheme met with some favour, although in the end it was dropped on grounds of expense. Once again Garibaldi was disappointed with parliament.

Indeed, by this time, Garibaldi had lost all hope that parliamentary democracy would solve Italy's problems. He was disillusioned with the corruption that prevailed at all levels — in parliament, in the administration, in the army. The only ones who had gained from the unification of Italy were the rich and powerful; the poor, on the other hand, were more highly taxed than ever. The south in particular had suffered and he could not forget that this had been his gift to Italy.

The only solution to problems like these, he argued, was a benevolent dictator, elected by the people to rule for a limited period. Someone who could govern with love . . . as he had governed Sicily and Naples. Garibaldi's ideas always took account of practical needs, even if he sometimes did not think through all the consequences.

Throughout the last years of his life he continued to bombard the public with suggestions for curing the world of its evils, just as he often sent his advice to parliament without appearing in person. He gave the impression of being angry and bad-tempered, though in private life he had grown almost serene, resigned to the illness that now confined him almost entirely to a wheelchair.

Increasingly his thoughts were for his family, for which he needed to provide. A good deal of money, in the form of gifts, had come his way since 1860, but the struggle to create a farm on Caprera had eaten up almost everything. He needed also to help Menotti and Ricciotti, both of whom had incurred debts.

Time and again he had refused a pension from the state. "I have never been poor", he protested, "because I have always cut my coat according to my cloth." This he meant even on a literal level, sometimes having no more than one change of shirt!

Finally, when a liberal government came to power in 1874, Garibaldi gave in and accepted a sum of money from the State. He felt a genuine sense of shame. "I never thought I would be reduced to the state of a pensioner!" he told Jessie White Mario. Perhaps to ease his conscience, he got rid of most of it as quickly as possible. Some was even lent to an old friend to save a shipping company from bankruptcy.

Another problem to be resolved before his death was how to make his three children by Francesca legitimate. He asked both parliament and the king to dissolve the marriage he had contracted with Giuseppina Raimondi in 1860. The king, who had illegitimate children of his own, was amused. "How can I help you", he had asked, "when there is nothing I can do to help myself!"

In the end, however, Garibaldi managed to get the marriage dissolved in 1880 and a few days later, on January 26, he and Francesca, surrounded by their children, were married on Caprera.

In the last few years he had seen many of his friends and enemies go to their graves before him. Mazzini, who in the course of his life had been both a friend and an enemy, had come back to Italy shortly before his death in 1872. When Garibaldi heard the news, he sent a telegram to Genoa saying: 'Let the flag of the Thousand fly over the bier of the great Italian.' He did not, however, attend Mazzini's funeral himself.

Pius IX had also died, and so had his adviser, Cardinal Antonelli. Rattazzi and La Marmora were also dead and in 1878 King Victor Emmanuel died too. Garibaldi must have felt that his own end would not be long in coming.

In the spring of 1882, he decided to pay a final visit to Sicily, which he had not seen since 1862, shortly before Aspromonte. His reason was to attend the ceremony of the Sicilian Vespers, which celebrated the uprising in which the Sicilians had thrown out their Norman rulers.

Carried on a stretcher, he was almost too weak to acknowledge the cheers of the people, who, whatever they had suffered since then at the hands of an uncaring government, had never forgotten the hero who had driven out the Neapolitans. But on the day he was too ill even to attend the ceremony, giving rise to the rumour that this feeble old man could not be the invincible Garibaldi.

On his return to Caprera, he began to suffer increasingly from bronchitis and by the end of May his breathing had become so difficult that it was clear he had little time left to live. Telegrams were sent to summon Menotti and Teresita.

Francesca had moved his bed so that he could see the sea, which had always given him pleasure to look at even while he was in prison. When a ship passed, he asked if it was bringing his children and, on the last afternoon, two finches came and settled on the window-sill. "Don't drive them away," he said. "They are the souls of my two daughters, come to fetch me."

Shortly afterwards, at six thirty in the evening, he died. It was June 2, a month before his seventy-fifth birthday.

Garibaldi had given Francesca orders that he should be burnt on a funeral pyre, dressed in his red shirt under the open sky. It was an idea that had taken his fancy when he heard Jessie White Mario describe the funeral of Shelley, who had been burnt on the sea-shore, and no doubt it reminded him of the way the Greek heroes

110

had made their exit. He had left precise instructions how it should be done.

Francesca had also been told to delay announcing his death for a few days so that his body could be burnt before the State intervened.

But in the end the State had its way. At a council of family and friends it was argued that Garibaldi belonged to Italy and therefore he must be given a proper funeral, and buried with all the honours due to him — honours which he had often been denied during his lifetime. The king was represented by his son and the presidents of both chambers attended, as well as other distinguished men. Survivors of the Thousand carried his coffin to the grave among the vines.

It was a moving ceremony. Only the weather, in the form of a violent thunderstorm, expressed its disapproval of the occasion.

24

A Calendar of the Main Events in the Life of Garibaldi

1807   Born in Nice (part of France until 1814) on July 4.

1824–33 Works as merchant seaman in the Mediterranean and the Black Sea.

1825   Sees Rome for the first time.

1831   Gets master's certificate.

1833   Comes in contact with Saint-Simonians and with Mazzini's 'Young Italy', which he joins on return to Marseilles.
Joins navy to do military service (December).

1834   Involved in attempted naval mutiny in Genoa (February).
Escapes to Nice and then to Marseilles.
Works as seaman in the Black Sea and the Mediterranean.

1835   Emigrates to Rio de Janeiro (September).
Age: 28.

1836   Joins local branch of 'Young Italy' and establishes contact with Mazzini.
Works as trader.

1837–41 Fights for the province of Rio Grande do Sul (in revolt from Brazil) as 'pirate' and guerrilla fighter.

1839   Meets Anita in Laguna (and later marries her in Montevideo in 1842).

1841   Leaves for Montevideo and works as teacher and trader.
Age: 34.

1842–48 Fights for the Uruguayans in their war against Argentina.

1842   Leads naval expedition up the Paraná. Battle of Costa Brava (August).

1843   Forms and commands Italian legion.

1846   Fights Battle of San Antonio (February).

Begins to think of returning to Italy, where reforms are taking place.

1848   Returns with part of Italian legion to Italy — and arrives (June) to find that revolution has broken out in Europe. Fights guerrilla war in north Italy (July–August) but in the end forced to retreat to Switzerland.
While going to fight in Venice (November), learns of revolution in Rome following the assassination of Count Rossi.
Age: 41.

1849   Plays major part in the defence of the Roman republic. Defeats first French attack on Rome (April) and defeats Neapolitans at Velletri (May).
Fights further battles against French (June).
Leads volunteers on retreat from Rome (July).
Anita dies on August 4 near Comacchio.
Escapes across Italy and returns to Chiavari, where he is arrested and sent into exile (September).

1850   After spending seven months at Tangier, where he writes memoirs, goes to New York (July).
Does manual work in factory.

1851–53 Works as captain of merchant ship and travels from South America to China and Australia.

1854   Returns from exile to Italy (May).
While passing through London (February), meets Mazzini but declines to become involved in revolutionary plots.
Briefly engaged to English woman, Emma Roberts.
Age: 46.

1854–59 Lives quietly with his family.
Works briefly as coastal trader but in 1855 buys part of the island of Caprera, where he builds a house and starts farming.

1856   Involved in scheme to rescue Neapolitan political prisoners, which is abandoned when boat wrecked.

1858   Meets Cavour, who is plotting war against Austria with Louis Napoleon, and is drawn back into politics.

1859   Made general in Piedmontese army (March) and forms volunteer army.
War breaks out with Austria (April). Austrians are defeated, with French help, at Magenta and Solferino (June).

In the course of the war, fights successful engagements with his volunteers.

After peace made, involved in plans to invade Papal States; then returns to private life.

1860   Although already has daughter by housekeeper/mistress Battistina, marries Giuseppina Raimondi (January), but abandons her on wedding day.

As deputy for Nice, attacks Cavour (April) for ceding Nice and Savoy to France.

Becomes involved in plot to liberate Sicily from the Neapolitans and leads expedition of 'The Thousand' (May).

Defeats Neapolitans at Calatafimi and captures Palermo (May).

Rules Sicily as 'dictator' (June–July) and then crosses to mainland (August).

Enters Naples and becomes 'dictator' (September).

After battle of Volturno (October), hands over power to King Victor Emmanuel (November) and retires to Caprera. Age: 53.

1861   Attacks Cavour over treatment of volunteers (April).
Death of Cavour.

1862   Leaves Caprera for Sicily (June) and raises volunteer army. Crosses to the mainland with the intention of marching on Rome, but is defeated and badly wounded at Aspromonte (August).

Is imprisoned, and then returns to Caprera (December).

1864   Visits England (April), where he is triumphantly received, but cuts visit short.

1866   Leads volunteer army in war against the Austrians (June–August). Austrians defeat Italians at Custoza and Lissa.
Age: 59
Venice becomes part of Italy.

1867   Agitates for war to make Rome capital of a united Italy. Raises volunteer army, with help of sons, but is arrested and sent back to Caprera (September).

Escapes from Caprera (October), marches on Rome but is defeated at Mentana (November).

Arrested and sent back to Caprera.

1868–69 Lives quietly on Caprera, writing and farming.

1870	Fights on behalf of republican France after Louis Napoleon is defeated by Prussians.
	Italians occupy Rome (September) after French troops withdrawn.
	Given command of 'The Army of the Vosges' (November–January).
	Age: 63
1871	After armistice (January) returns to quiet life on Caprera. Writes final version of memoirs.
1875	Visits Rome. Takes seat in parliament and becomes involved in scheme for changing course of the Tiber.
1880	Finally secures divorce from Giuseppina Raimondi (January) and marries Francesca Armosino, by whom he has children.
1882	Visits Sicily for anniversary of Sicilian Vespers (March–April).
	On his return falls ill (May) and dies on June 2, a month before his seventy-fifth birthday.

Select Bibliography

Many thousands of books and articles have been written about Garibaldi. The majority of these are in Italian, but a considerable number are in English. The short list of books below is intended as a guide for the general reader who is interested in finding out more about Garibaldi. It includes only books likely to be reasonably easily obtainable (at least in libraries). Of these the book by John Parris is the most entertaining, while the one by Jasper Ridley is the most comprehensive. Ridley's bibliography will also provide a guide to the wide range of works on Garibaldi in English, Italian and Spanish, although new books are continually being produced. Garibaldi's own memoirs have not been recently translated.

Denis Mack Smith   *Garibaldi, A Great Life In Brief* (Knopf 1956, reissued by The Greenwood Press 1982)

John Parris   *The Lion of Caprera* (Barker 1962)

Christopher Hibbert   *Garibaldi and his Enemies* (Longman 1965)

Jasper Ridley   *Garibaldi* (Constable 1974)